THE QUEST OF FAITH

THE QUEST OF FAITH

An introduction to contemporary religions

by

JOHN H. CHAMBERLAYNE

M.A., Ph.D (Lond.)

THE RELIGIOUS EDUCATION PRESS LIMITED

(A member of the Pergamon Group)

HEADINGTON HILL HALL   OXFORD

THE RELIGIOUS EDUCATION PRESS LTD

(A member of the Pergamon Group)

OXFORD · LONDON · EDINBURGH
NEW YORK · TORONTO · SYDNEY

Copyright © 1969 John H. Chamberlayne
First edition 1969
Library of Congress Catalog Card No. 73–84069

Printed in Great Britain by A. Wheaton & Co., Exeter

08 006515 5 (flexicover)
08 006889 8 (hard cover)

TO
JOHN
BARBARA
AND
DAVID

PREFACE

THE study of the religions of the world has ceased to be merely the academic interest of a few specialists, who want to know more about the beliefs of the people who live 'over there' in Africa, India and China. It is no longer a matter of academic interest when the bus-drivers of Birmingham come out on strike due to trouble over a Sikh employee, who for religious reasons wears a turban or a beard, which he is unwilling to remove at the request of the bus company. The very large number of newcomers from overseas have brought their beliefs and practices into British society, so that it is needful to seek some clearer understanding of their ways and their beliefs.

The chapters of this book endeavour to describe simply the great religions of the world, showing their historical development and also their impact on our own culture at this time. It is important to give due place to the social implications of a religion in its own culture and in new cultures as it enters them. I have tried to give as balanced a picture as possible, with scientific respect for facts, without thereby acting falsely to my own convictions.

Reference will be found at the close of the book to two subjects, which are important aspects of religion and worthy of considerable exploration; hence their place as appendixes. Further study in the various religions will be assisted by the books found in the Bibliography.

The religious search has been very widespread and continuous. A deeper understanding between peoples can spring from a sharing of beliefs and values, so that truth may shine in its own light and faith may be illumined by the insights given to all mankind.

J. H. CHAMBERLAYNE.

Muswell Hill.

Easter. 1969.

CONTENTS

I

INTRODUCTION

I. Where did the Quest begin?

The earliest cultures known to mankind show evidence that man was curious about his environment, that he was aware that mystery surrounded his life from start to finish and that it was necessary for him to seek ways to live in harmony with the great forces (natural and otherwise) which surrounded him. The mysteries of creation and the struggle for survival were so overwhelming that, since earliest times, every resource was welcome which could help man to triumph over Nature. From the cave dwellings of the Stone Age and the later hunting cultures, there is seen the pictorial representations of bison and stag whose capture meant survival for the families of the hunters. These representations were not merely pictures but were also religious in intent—as they served as the pleas of these peoples for power from the hunting spirits to enable the hunters to shoot straight and true to the hearts of these animals.

Not only did the desire for survival in terms of food call forth a quest of faith. The need for the survival of the group made birth an experience which was an object of fear yet of fascination. Every new experience was an excursion in faith; every new member had to face tests for initiation into the community and each new enterprise had to be faced with a sense of awe. The sense of inner connection at the heart of all things gave rise to a belief in Providence, expressed in the instincts of self-preservation, of sex and of group solidarity. The term 'religion' arose in the Latin peoples with the meaning of two kinds, on which scholars have long been sharply divided.

On the one hand, the Roman writer Cicero believed that the word (in Latin *religio*) came from a stem or root *leg*, meaning 'to collect or to observe', so 'to observe signs of divine communication to men', whilst another Roman writer Servius held that it came from another root, *lig* (meaning 'to bind'), so that the term *religio* meant 'that which binds, a relationship', in this case, between the human and the more-than-human, whether in Nature or seen in more personal forms, as a deity. St. Augustine of Hippo (died A.D. 430) used the term in both senses—each of which raises interesting issues. On the one hand, the careful observation of omens and ritual has been regarded as the essence of religion, whilst, on the other, there has been the recognition that an inner communion (not outward ceremony) is of the essential nature of religion.

2. How has the Quest been pursued?

In different cultures, whether among early hunters, varying tribal communities, the agricultural civilisations, or great urban centres—the shape of society, its standards and practices have both been determined by and have helped to determine the religious life of the people. The study of different religions is related to many factors, including geography, history, trade, war and personal ambitions, which serve to supplement the vision of the prophet, the correct ritual of the priest and the oratory of preacher and evangelist. In fact, it may well be claimed that religion has served as the wider hypothesis which seeks to embrace the hypotheses of all other departments of life to provide meaning and integration to the whole. This has been expressed in a different way by the anthropologist, whose work has emphasised the 'function' of religion in integrating the social life of tribes. The arrival of the Westerner, with new values and practices (whether traders, government officials or missionaries), can cause a break-up of a community, whose beliefs and customs have been very closely interwoven and whose 'way of life' was thereby fully integrated. Any departure from the norm, without the replacement of a suitable alternative norm, inevitably throws the life of the community into chaos.

At the same time, the recognition of certain definite norms provides, not only the community, but also the individual with an integration of character, as the psycho-analyst has shown in many cases of mental disturbance. Such an integration, for the individual, may centre around a variety of objects—wealth, power over people, some steadfast cause as well as an instinct such as fear. Such integration, however, may be seen to have a greater power when it is shared in a community which holds beliefs and practices in common, which reinforce those of the individual. It is therefore with the close inter-relationship between these two forms of integration that this quest has to be seen.

In the history of the quest for faith, social factors have played an important part but so too have those prophetic individuals whose teaching has acted as a focus for their followers. It is always a fascinating issue to discuss the relationship between an individual prophet and the life of his time. The word of the prophet rings a bell which continues to sound long after he has died. His personality and its impact on his immediate followers, as well the interpretations given to his teaching by later writers, all serve to shape the course of communities, the customs of families and the worship of believers. Some paths of faith have proved fruitless and been abandoned, whilst others have spread far beyond their land of origin.

Moreover, it is not always easy to discover the precise form that religion may take in a particular age and culture. For example, it is customary in the West (e.g. in Europe) to think of 'religion' as a form of fixed relationship between man and the Sacred, the Absolute, or simply, 'God'. However, east of Suez it is more usual to describe the quest as 'the Way'—in early Christianity, in Judaism, in Buddhism (with its 'noble eight-fold Path') and in Japanese Shintoism (in which Shinto is 'the Way of the Gods'); while even though Communism may reject belief in God (theism) yet it still describes the Dialectical Process as 'the Way'. It is noteworthy that throughout there lies a belief in some direction whether in terms of Process rather than with a Person—and this direction is believed to be in the highest interests of human life. It may well be that the conception of Divine Mind may not be present but the desire for inner harmony may well call for some such conception as a link between the inner and outer order.

As greater stores of material become available through archaeology, anthropology and sociology as well as in the wider study of the comparative history of religions, it is less easy to channel such material into easily accessible forms. It is, nevertheless, needful to have sufficient to give light on present religious paths, especially when, through immigration and increasing cultural contacts, others' beliefs and practices are coming into contact with native British ones. The Indian students who study in Britain naturally wish to honour their own practices and it is important in the process of understanding to have some insight into the history and meaning of such practices. The forms of religion which arise in new social conditions in Japan throw light on human needs and the ways in which religious faith has made provision for such needs.

In the chapters of this book, certain paths of religious faith have been chosen. These paths are all trodden by millions of followers today and therefore have living relevance for contemporary culture. They have a particular history which gives them their own characteristics which are important in the task of understanding others. These faiths have resulted in different cultures, which are now coming into closer contact with one another. But moving closer to new people (or to a new culture) does not automatically ensure good neighbourliness. Good relations depend on a willingness to share and understand one another.

Therefore, in each chapter, after an introduction in regard to the history of the particular religion, there follows some brief account of the practices and outlook of that religion. At the close of each chapter, there is a short appraisal of the impact of our own culture on those from India, Africa or Islam, with the reactions of these other believers to their treatment here. For example, in the Welfare State in Britain, many British people are proud of the care and the homes provided for elderly people, who otherwise would live in great loneliness.

On the other hand, many Indians and Chinese who come to British shores are shocked by the failure of families to care for their own old people but leave such provision to a Welfare State. The outlook of those who have grown up under the shadow of great respect for ancestors is very different from those who have grown up within a culture in which Christian beliefs have played a large part. The cults of ancestors give a very different outlook from one which believes in the Communion of Saints and the Church Triumphant. The clash of cultures is made more violent when the outward phenomena of race and colour are also present. The cultural differences become more deeply endorsed and thereby the conflict possibilities are increased.

There are naturally limitations in seeking to compact so much into so small a compass. The study of the religions of India would by itself require a large volume or a large number of volumes, especially if the background of the religion were to receive adequate treatment. For example, in Bombay there is the large community of Parsees, whose religion has a long history which stretches back to Zarathustra. To do justice to the religion of the Parsees, it would need some attention to be paid to this long period of historical development.

The attempt in this book is more modest. It simply seeks to give a brief account of the religion which is practised by its adherents today. A short Bibliography at the end gives reference to some further works for those who wish to pursue the quest further. The study of religion is more than the collection of religions, since the search by man to find the supernatural and eternal in the day-to-day duties glows with fascinating fervour among all races. It is also difficult to enter with sufficient humility into religions which are not one's own. Practices which may seem crude and superstitious may form part of an institutional framework, which at the same time gives room for highly intellectual conceptions of the universe and of man. However, the endeavour to explore the religious quest of mankind is both fascinating and fruitful if such a quest opens the way to deeper insights into the nature of men and of nations and, perchance, into the nature of God Himself.

II

PRE-LITERARE RELIGION

1. Introduction

The nature of prehistoric religion is lost in obscurity. Its roots lay in the seed-bed of human consciousness, in the awareness of relationship to and dependence on the whole natural order. The awareness of relationship found expression in numerous folk tales in which children were suckled by wolves and even of kinship with snakes and kangaroos, in forms of totemism. The sense of dependence centred round three main instinctive urges—self-preservation, the continuance of the species and the survival of the group. From very humble beginnings, the religious sentiment arose with the conception of a supernatural power or Providence, as a source of re-creative life and of the ordering of social life.

It is not clear how far we can reconstruct knowledge of early religious belief and practice—from the beliefs of the lowest and least developed peoples still in existence; from certain archaeological findings and from genetic psychology. Three main views have been supported by scholars, namely, that early man believed in a supernatural power (*mana*), which pervaded all nature but was particularly manifest in unusual objects (wind, fire, chiefs, powerful weapons, dwarfs, etc.); that man first believed in a theory of spirits (animism) which in-dwelt objects which aroused his curiosity and thirdly, that early man had a belief in high gods (a primitive monotheism), of which there are survivals in the legends of many peoples of all cultures until today. However religion arose, it has shown various facets which appear in religious life at all levels of social existence.

Behind these facets, there is evident a desire for harmony in man's existence, that is, an endeavour to give meaning and purpose to himself, his environment and the wider transcendental order as well as to avoid conflict between these elements. His survival as a family, a group or as a wider community depended on this harmony. If he could learn the way to co-operate with Nature, long before he could hope to 'master' it, then his livelihood was more likely to be ensured. To this end, he practised certain observances, which he believed would show his longing for harmony.

2. Religious Practice

These observances came to be clear facets of the religious life and included sacrifice, prayer and other rituals, which took place within the communal setting of his life. Sacrifice took a variety of forms and has become a common feature of most religions. It has often taken the form of a gift which has been dedicated to the god by killing (as in the case of an animal), by burning or (in the case of fluids) by being poured out. A number of motives have been present in most sacrifices and include adoration, thanksgiving, bargaining, propitiation (as with a peace offering) and expiation (to provide reparation or compensation). Even in the case of adoration, there are mixed intentions—as many such offerings were believed to be needful to keep the gods alive.

Many offerings were intended to keep capricious demons quiet and avoid their molestation. Thanksgiving has also continued to have a prominent place, from early times, as may be seen from the gifts made to tree spirits (in China, India and Africa), whose beneficent offices have been deemed active in healing and helping. It is not easy to discover the most prominent motive in sacrifice, but it may well have been to ensure the continuance of the good offices of a benevolent power, sometimes conceived as a kind of 'elderly parent', who presides over the well-being of his children. This is evident in the little earth-gods and spirits who serve in this way in the Chinese countryside.

Sacrifices have often been regarded as destroying life (whether by killing or burning or driving away), yet such actions need to be seen as ways of *releasing* life for the benefit of the deity as well as seeking to please. If the odour of incense provides pleasure to human nostrils then sweet perfumes will provide pleasure for the 'higher powers'. In the case of animal sacrifices, there is involved both the value of the offering and the sharing of life. The sheep or goat is a valued part of the flock and so it is a costly offering. But in the shedding of blood, there is a bond between the deity and the worshippers just as, in human contracts, the use of blood was a symbol of the solemnity of the contract. When the sacrifice of blood takes the form of a communion meal, then the actual life of the animal is shared with the deity, who has his portion, just as the worshippers have theirs.

There is a wide diversity in sacrifice. It may be a simple offering to invoke power, especially for one's livelihood. 'He sacrificeth unto his net, and burneth incense unto his drag; because by them his portion is fat, and his meat plenteous' (Habakkuk *1*. 16), so the Hindu today, in the festival of Ayudah Puja, offers flowers, incense, and at times a kid, to the tools of his profession, including his motor-cycle. Yet sacrifice may take the form of an act of self-abandonment before the Most High in utter contrition and adoration.

Perhaps the most common view of sacrifice is that of 'tit-for-tat', a form of bargain. 'If you will provide a son or protection, then I will offer such and such gifts.' In such cases, it is clear that the deity is approached to be made use of, as Professor Leuba contended, just as senior officials are approached by lower officials. The nature of the conception of sacrifice is closely linked with the character of the god and is enhanced with the spirituality of the god.

Sacrifice is normally a form of ritual, an external act to express an inward intention. Ritual plays a very large part in pre-literate religion and is far wider than the act of sacrifice. It includes the many forms of physical activity by which devotion to and union with the deity are expressed. There is the use of the dance as a re-enactment of fertility and creation rites, whether among Red Indians in North America or among Bantu tribesmen in Africa. Gifts to the goddess as a simple token of piety may be a ritual act, before an examination, in India and China. On a larger scale, ritual drama may serve to draw a wider community together in re-enactment of their history. They are reminded afresh of their common bonds.

Ritual acts, even among non-literate peoples, are seldom alone. They are normally accompanied by some form of verbal expression, known as 'myth'. The myth seeks to give verbal explanation or interpretation of the deed enacted, especially in drama. In earlier times, in Babylonia, the New Year Festival was a renewal of the land, by a sacred drama in word and action. Word may take the form of a legend, such as the Babylonian Epic of Creation, which was annually recited on the fourth day of the New Year's festival. Often it has taken the form of ballads, which were sung in the fields but were unwritten among peoples who had no writing or literature of their own.

Such were the ballads which are still sung among the A-Hsi, who are a small tribe of the Yi group, who belong to the Lolo people, one of the major tribes in West China. 'The Creation Story of the A-Hsi', which was translated by W. H. Hudspeth, is a collection of ballads on creation, on soil cultivation and the course of true love. These songs handed on the beliefs and culture of such tribal peoples from generation to generation.

3. The Use of Myth

The importance of the myth lies in the fact that the recitation of the story is regarded as an operational part of the actual event, so that if the repetition of the legend does not take place, then the desired event (e.g. fertility) will not take place. At the same time, the myth also serves as a means of explanation for events in Nature and in human life, when actual historical and factual knowledge is lacking. A tribe or city, in an early stage of culture, may know little about atmospherics and the movements of the winds, yet they are aware that great clouds do cover the sun and as the clouds gather, rain comes—for which the picture of a great bird, with outstretched wings, blotting out the sun is not an altogether inadequate description. Reasons for the action of such a great bird naturally follow in the form of a a legend. Examples of such myths in earlier times may be found in S. H. Hooke's *Middle East Mythology* (Penguin, 1963), in which the various types of myth (of ritual; of origin; of the cult, etc.) are indicated. Among tribal peoples today, such myths abound as the investigations of the cultural anthropologists and of missionaries show.

The *ritual* consisted of the part that was enacted or done, while the *myth* was the part that was spoken. This spoken part took a variety of forms. It was often in the form of a connected story. Sometimes it took the form of a chant or an incantation. In either case, the magical efficacy of the spoken word was regarded as an essential part of the ritual. As S. H. Hooke points out, 'the story was not told to amuse an audience; it was a word of power. The repetition of the magic words had power to bring about, or recreate, the situation which they described' (p. 12). This spoken word developed into further ritual acts, namely, the use of the prayer and the spell as means to approach a deity.

4. Spell and Prayer

The study of cultural anthropologists, like Malinowski, has made clear that pre-literate (or primitive) man is not pre-logical or mystical in his approach to the world around him. A distinction is made between those tasks which the tribal man can perform by his own technical knowledge and skill and those which require the help of wider resources.

Herein lies the distinction also between the spell and the prayer. A belief in powers or a power more than human lies behind both the spell and the prayer. It is recognised that this more than human power needs to be invoked for the successful result in an enterprise. But some activities are more routine and well-known than others. The growth of the crops follows a clearly recognised pattern from season to season. The knowledge of seeds, the weather conditions, soils and other technical matters are realised to have importance but still the greater powers need to be invoked. These invocations have in many cases the form of spells—a form of words to promote the fertility of the crops.

Yet this form has become so routinised that it is formal beyond words. It may be regarded as not merely an invocation but an attempt to compel the spirits to carry out their task. The use of powerful names of gods or spirits, the forms of language connected with the use of various tools, and power or *mana* in certain words—all serve to make the spell a powerful influence in many parts of the world today.

The Australian aborigines, the village elders in many Indian villages and among the Bantu peoples of South Africa, are examples of peoples among whom the spell exercises a great control in their day-to-day affairs at the present time. As a form of magic, the spell is in fact a form of coercion, to exercise a power over certain spirits who have an influence on the welfare of a project. The spell is intended to use the deity to serve one's private or public purposes (for good or ill), which contrasts with the use of prayer which seeks the assistance of the deity in situations which are beyond the worshippers' control. Thus, as Malinowski has pointed out, the Trobriand Islander uses magic when he fishes in inland lagoons (which he knows and where he can in large measure have control) but uses prayer and religious exercises when he goes to fish beyond the reef in the open sea, where he has no such control. This constituted the early differentiation between the sphere of magic (which seeks to control (even to manipulate) the deity) and that of religion (which implores the assistance of the deity).

In approaching the deity, prayer as a mental exercise has taken many forms. In early times, as men lived in close corporate life, prayer was generally public. When paleolithic man went hunting, he sought supernatural power to assist him, using rituals and invocations for the purpose. The rituals are depicted in the inner recesses of caves as in Niaux in Ariège and in the animal disguises as Trois Frères, near St. Girons in the French Pyrenees. The invocations were no doubt simple requests, which became elaborated with time, as may be seen from the prayers of the Todas, one of the most primitive peoples of modern India.

It is not difficult for a form of words to become formalised and stereotyped. This is evident in the early religious history of India, in which the spontaneous prayers of the early Rishis have become crystallised into magical form in Brahmanism. The prayer-wheel of the Tibetan, the Sanskrit prayer for the illiterate Hindu, the Pali prayer of the Chinese Buddhist and even the Christian Pater Noster show the same tendency. Yet, despite these dangers, varied expressions of prayer have emerged in all religions to communicate with the deity.

Variety in prayer has arisen because it has its place in private as well as public worship, with subjective and objective aspects. The strong social bonds of primitive society have been stressed and these bonds have been strengthened by communal rituals and prayers but it is apparent that, at the same time, private prayer has also a place in pre-literate community life as certain individuals have made their way to quiet groves to pour out their souls to some more-than-human Power. There is little doubt that in such communities there are the mystics and shamen who seek communion with higher powers or believe themselves to be able to communicate with such powers. Such prayers, whether private or public, have a subjective aspect in their reflective communion with the Divine but, in early religion, there is a large objective element, to address the deity as distinct from oneself. The more reflective aspect of religion appears with the rising level of human culture.

The purpose of such prayer remains similar in all stages of culture. External causes and the functions it performs both bear a part. The external causes lie in the instruction of the elders and in the example of others which the younger generation follow. The functions it performs arise out of a sense of need. This need differs widely, ranging from a dire strait for food for survival to a far-reaching desire to find harmony with the creative Being whose life embraces all things. The very limitations of human thought and knowledge give rise to a sense of insufficiency. Human weakness and insecurity seek to find a path to the 'All-Knowing', who may be the 'All-Loving' too; a beneficent Power able to help the groping endeavours of mankind, an all-embracing Providence. Scepticism, ill-health and the sense of separation or sin may cause men to cease from prayer, but it remains as a leading factor in religious practice.

The use of prayer is often verbal and it is probable that the most ancient form is that of blessing or cursing. Such a word of power depends frequently on the person who utters it. Among the early hunters there was the 'shaman', a strange prophetic person, who gave guidance to his family or his people in times of need. He is found today in the person of the 'witch-doctor', who is believed to have influence over the spirits, so that at times he may command their help. The influence of the sacred person is very widespread and is found in all religions. Strange nervous, even neurotic, symptoms were believed to mark out those who had been chosen by the divine powers for this office. Among the Cherokee Red Indians, the medicine man is recognized by such symptoms as a late birth, certain nervous ticks and other unusual signs, which are acknowledged by the members of his tribe. He is regarded as a channel of communication with the spirits, who guide him to divine and tell fortunes. He has to maintain right and harmonious relations between the community and the divine powers.

5. The Sacred Person

The place of this sacred person is important for a number of reasons. In a highly communal society, this individual will be marked out and even shunned, so that he may be compelled to be a solitary soul. This was one path to the rise of individualism. Such a person also was often meditative and communed with nature in lonely places, hence arose the mystic which resulted in India in the exaltation of the solitary life. In places, this 'sacred man' had the company of others, so that a stratum in society arose, a specialised social class to deal with moral and religious issues. Such sacred men in due time became differentiated into those who were prophets and those who were priests. The former appear to be the earlier, as the prophet was regarded as the direct communicator with the divine, while the priest rationalised the communications thus received.

The task of this sacred person is varied. It includes the interpretation of dreams, the recognition of omens (which embraces a wide knowledge of natural phenomena, e.g. the flight and habits of birds), the settlement of disputes between individuals and groups, as well as a knowledge of the suitable rituals for all possible occasions. A hunting trip, a marriage, the celebration of a birth as well as the 'passing' of a member of the group are occasions when such rituals (known as the *rites de passage*) need to be carried out. Such knowledge is sometimes passed from father to son or from uncle to nephew, as a form of secret skill which is the preserve of the family. Oftimes, the holy man is an ascetic and is marked out by a strange appearance, perhaps a hunchback, or forms of fits and wild behaviour, which is liable to create a sense of awe among his fellows who especially go to seek him out in time of need.

His power lies in his ability to provide insight (he was often called a 'seer') into the divine order, by his skills in retaining harmony with that order and by the social harmony which prevailed from this means of coping with public and personal anxieties. It is noteworthy that the sacred man had, in most communities, a place close to the chief. He had a ready access to the presence and the counsels of the chief and he could be a great helper in approaching the chief in important matters. In the use of his powers (for good or ill), even the chief believed that he had to deal with respect with the sacred man, lest the spirits whom that holy man represented became offended and brought disaster upon the community. This strange figure has retained his influence in a very remarkable way in the life of Islam. He has 'charismatic' (special gifts from the extraordinary order) powers and needs to be respected on that account.

The actions of such men were not haphazard. They took place at special times and in particular places. The recognition of the earth cycle, with the changing seasons, is found in most cultures. There are in fact three cycles, those of heaven, earth and human life. In his endeavour to maintain harmony, the hunter and agriculturalist saw religious significance in the use of the calendar. In Ancient Egypt, one-fifth of the days of the years were sacred days, when work was prohibited, while in Republican Rome, one-third of the days of the year were *dies nefasti* (unlawful days), which were days of danger to the community.

Among primitive peoples, these sacred days or seasons normally took place during the periods of leisure and waiting, e.g. while the harvest was awaited or when the sun was about to return. These were times of anxiety, lest the crop failed or the light ceased, when pent-up emotions found expression in dances and displays, with acts of sympathetic magic. This is seen in the case of the Yule period, with the great fires, to encourage the sun to return. Most early cultures have a year-end festival, especially during the period in which the solar year and the lunar year overlap (known in the Christian year as the period of Epiphany or the Twelve Days after Christmas).

During the festive days, the deeds of heroes were recited, the activities of the gods were recollected and drama used to depict the hopes of the people. These festivities are very marked in the agriculturalist's year, with a ritual cycle of events, to mark the various stages. The same use of a period of anxiety as one of ceremony (with religious purpose) is seen in the ceremonies which marked the events of birth, adolescence, marriage and the mourning of death. These were spiritual events of the greatest significance to the individual, the family and society in general.

6. Sacred Times

These special times still have their significance as the Christian Church has its sacred calendar, setting apart certain days of peculiar importance in the course of the years. The ancient idea that earth and heaven need to keep in harmony is also reflected in the popular magazines which give horoscopes of the various divisions of the year, which is deemed to act in accord with various divisions of the heavenly constellations. With the movements of the stars, the actions of mortals are believed to have some form of moral relationship, as the Babylonians, the Persian Magi and later astrologers have claimed. It is evident that the movements in the heavens, particularly the action of the moon, aroused interest, if not concern, amongst many primitive peoples, who used the moon's phases as the method to mark out the periods of the month.

With the rise of gods and goddesses, the practice of marking out their birthdays and special festival days became common. Special times gave the opportunity to rekindle devotion to the object of worship and often occasion to refurbish the shrine, which was visited, cleaned and redecorated. This took place and, in fact, continues to do so, on the first and fifteenth of the month, in China and India. In the Near East, the seventh day had particular significance as specially exposed to danger. This has been replaced in the Christian Calendar by the first day of the week, which is the celebration of the Resurrection of the Lord Jesus. The Christian Festivals often cover some earlier festivals, generally agricultural in origin. It is, in fact, probable that a number of early festivals lie beneath the celebration of Christmas at the close of the year. Thus, time is seen to be sacred and its use needed to be ordered with deliberation and care.

7. Sacred Places

The activities of sacred persons, at the special times, were often centred on particular places, which were believed to have a significance of their own. The 'high-place' is found in most religions. Among the tribes who swept into early Greece, the gods dwelt in the mountains in the north (Olympus). In Palestine, the high places were the centres of sacrifice among the Canaanites. The high mountain served as a peak of veneration, so that there are the Five Peaks of Taoism and the Five Mountains of Buddhism in China.

In the pre-literate stage, the sacred place is often a grove or secluded place, where the spirits are believed to have their abode. Such a place may be focused in an ancient tree, whose presence is immemorial and whose shade has been the centre of communal affairs for as long as the oldest members of the community can remember. Thus, among the Israelite tribes, the prophetess Deborah sat beneath a palm tree to deliver her judgments. In many parts of China, ancient trees have become objects of veneration, even though the trees may have long been swept away but their stump has remained. Objects of respect, boards of thanksgiving and various tokens of gratitude are placed around the stump. Such a place is considered to have power (*mana*) of its own. Decisions taken at such a spot have a particular effectiveness. Vows which are made there are very efficacious, while such places are renowned as centres for pronouncing blessings and cursings.

The later sanctuaries were often places which had earlier been those where 'numinous' experience had taken place. 'Numinous' experience was the awareness of the divine which came to be particularly associated with these places.

It is also interesting that the idea of sacred places came to be extended into the realm of the imagination, so that 'Sheo'ol' (the underworld) and the fields of Valhalla (for Aryan heroes) were sacred places in the realm of faith as 'countries of the soul'.

It seems probable that sacred images came into use at the time of the agricultural stage of culture. The early images may well have been representations of the spirit of vegetation. Female and male figures are found in early Indo-Aryan discoveries in North India. Some of them are simply pieces of wood or stone which represent some part of the human anatomy, expecially those which are connected with child-bearing. The figure may remain without significance, however, unless it is made effective by the consecration of a holy man, as in India, where an image is only quickened after it has been consecrated by a Brahmin priest. The spirit in the Chinese home or the clan temple only comes to dwell in the ancestral tablet after due ceremony. It is only with the further developments of culture, with improved techniques, that more elaborate images come to have a wider vogue. The figures in many Chinese shrines were probably very simple, if they existed at all until the advent of Buddhism in China, when the temples, the images and the ceremonies became far more elaborate.

Thus, in pre-literate religion, there were the elements which grew into wider use with the increased facilities which were available with the cultural development of humanity. The need for effective means to communicate with the divine was recognised as far back as we have any knowledge of man. Such means included the use of prayer and sacrifice, which could be more powerful, if they were performed by special persons, in special places, at particular times. The pattern of religious practice has widely differed but the need has called forth these common elements, which form part of the most advanced religious practice. Many experiments have been made in men's search for harmony with the divine and with man and these varieties in belief and practice express the diversity of the need.

Summary

The elements of pre-literate religion are important for more than one reason. They continue to be present as living elements in many lands where animism continues to flourish. In cultures, in which literacy has played a small part or is conspicuous by its absence, the symbolism and means of communication need to take other forms, so that the culture of the tribe may be transmitted. The safeguards to social life in the forms of taboos have to be clearly marked lest the community suffers as a whole. Therefore, the shrine, the fetish, the appointed time for first-fruits and the recognised medicine-man, are all important to ensure that the spirits will give their blessing or, contrariwise, will be prevented from creating havoc or harm.

But, at the same time, the human feeling of dependence on the wider powers in Nature and on those which control natural forces, created or discovered ways which proved so effectual that they have served as channels to be developed by later cultures. In this way, primitive man dug wells, which provided effectual means to quench not only his thirst but that of those who came after him. Some of these wells have become exhausted, or as beliefs are 'superstitions' (literally, 'left-overs'). Many of them have remained—in the use of sacred times, places and persons, who have enabled later saints and thinkers to travel further (to change the metaphor) along paths blazed by the earlier pioneers. There is a vast difference between the simple invocation of the village headman and the great prayers in the Mass, yet they spring from a common source and there is the same awareness of the need of divine help. The ways of development in different cultures are set forth in the following chapters.

III

RELIGION IN INDIA

1. Introduction

'India has examples of every conceivable type of attempt at the solution of the religious problem' (A. C. Bouquet). It is not a matter for surprise that many varieties of religious practice and belief are to be found in India, because there have been successive waves of invaders whose cultures have been imposed in layers upon earlier ones, one upon another. This has resulted in the survival of very primitive beliefs alongside profound philosophical conceptions.

In some places there are very primitive groups, such as the Andaman Islanders, who live in islands in the Bay of Bengal. Their culture and way of life is among the earliest known to mankind. Then, in the valley of the River Indus, in North India, there are the remains of a great Dravidian civilisation. The Dravidian peoples entered India about 2000 B.C. These people were small and dark-skinned. They were followed by waves of fair-skinned people, the Nordic Aryans, who were related to the Persians, and who established themselves in North India. These people came in successive waves and drove the earlier Dravidians further south.

In their desire to secure their supremacy and to prevent inter-marriage, the new ruling people imposed caste laws which made inter-marriage between groups not merely legally forbidden but religiously outlawed. Religious barriers were imposed between those of various occupations and social strata and these have remained until this day. There followed other invaders, such as the Mongols and the Scythians and, finally, the Moslem Arabs. All these invaders have influenced the religious beliefs and practices of India.

The Dravidians were mainly Nature worshippers, with tree worship, snake spirits and various fertility cults, some of which have in part survived until today. The belief in the snake as a sacred animal is very widespread, because it is regarded as long-lived (as it sheds its skin and is believed to renew its life) and is also associated with healing. The use of the snake in association with healing is seen in figures of healing gods and is remembered in the West, as the snake appears in the badge of the Royal Army Medical Corps.

The desire to have many children, so that the family group will survive, has made fertility cults popular. If a woman attends certain shrines on special days, it is believed that she will more probably bear a child. Often gifts are placed before the image of a particular goddess, so that she may be encouraged to show her favour by granting the gift of a child.

The Nordic invaders were similar to the Viking invaders in Northern Europe. They were hard fighters, ate well and drank deeply. They became the rulers in Northern India and their successors were the members of the highest castes among the Hindus. They sought to preserve their position by religious rites which separated various classes in society and prevented them from eating together and inter-marrying. From these peoples, there have come down the most ancient sacred books, the *Vedas*, which consist of hymns and poems, many of which are in honour of nature gods. They date from the period from 1500 to 800 B.C.

The earliest of the Vedas is the *Rig-Veda*, which is the most ancient source of Hinduism. This book has hymns addressed to parts of nature as gods, including the sun, the storm cloud, heaven, the wind, dawn and others. The deities associated with the sun are divided up into various divisions, such as Surya (the sun's disc), Savitar (the sun in its warmth), Vishnu (the sun in movement) and so on, in recognition of the sun's help.

This book contains 1028 hymns. The other Vedic books were compiled later, namely, the *Sama-Veda* (which consists of hymns used during sacrifice), the *Yajur-Veda* (which is a liturgy) and the *Atharva-Veda* (which mainly consists in charms and incantations). The materials which are found in these books probably were the result of developments which took place over several centuries. In these books, there is an idea of right relationships (*rita*) which covers several different aspects of life. It includes the order of nature, the moral order and human goodness, the holiness of the gods and also the use of sacrifice. The term *rita* is used to cover all these matters which were all regarded as expressions of a true way of righteousness. It is evident that during this period some thinkers had begun to think more deeply about the gods. There were also appearing some mystics, those who tried to find a technique which would bring them into closer inner union with the divine.

There followed a further literary period, from 800 B.C. to 500 B.C., when there was the Brahmanical period, during which the institutions of Hinduism developed. It is to this period that the Upanishads belong. This body of writings consists of some 250 items, which are varied in nature—including miscellaneous quotations, short hymns and notes and formulae, some 15 of which are the principal ones.

These writings show a further development of thought, moving away from the earlier belief in many gods towards an all-embracing Whole, known as *Brahma*. As the ground of existence, Brahma embraces all phenomena, all being and non-being. The human spirit or self is the *Atman* but this is essentially one in all selves, so individuality is in fact an illusion. The ideas of Brahma and Atman are identified, so that Deity is unknowable and all identity in things is illusion. This view of existence is known as 'monistic pantheism'.

It was during this period that the priests (the Brahmans) began to use the hymns as magical chants, and they considered that the very words of the Vedas were divine. As the sacrifices of the Brahmans were thought to be essential for the success of an enterprise (e.g. a marriage, a business contract, etc.), so the power of these priests steadily grew. There were several different ways of thought which grew out of this period.

The problem of evil is central to human experience. One solution, which came to be widely believed, was to claim that evil in one's present life was due to evil deeds which you had committed in a previous existence. This belief is known as *karma*. Your present suffering results from your actions in a previous cycle of existence. On the other hand, if you act well in your present existence, then there is the hope that in your next existence, you will have a better time. Thus it is believed that justice is worked out over a chain of existences. The major problem in this belief lies in the fact that you have no knowledge of your action in a previous existence, so you do not find relief in your present evil lot by a sense of repentance.

Linked to this belief in *karma*, there is also a belief that a person can return in a series of re-incarnations. He might return as another person or as some other form of life, as a dog or (if he is sly) as a fox. This belief in *samsara* also takes the form that the gods may come to share the lives of men, taking different forms.

Another form of thought is the belief that if you are able to achieve sufficient mastery over the physical desires and the body generally, then the spirit will have greater freedom. This is sought by *tapas* (or asceticism), of which an important aspect became known as *yoga*, the process of becoming yoked to the divine. The adept in this technique is a yogi, who uses a number of techniques and methods to secure intense concentration of mind and body. By taking up certain positions, using special breathing exercises, it is believed that he can produce a state of mystical contemplation. The desire to overcome natural desires is sought for various reasons. The techniques are believed to help the yogi to transcend in feeling the weary round of suffering (which is considered to be the destiny of all) and also to serve as a ladder by which the individual can be promoted to the next birth (or round of existence). It may be possible by such methods to be lifted to a higher and pleasanter form of life.

2. Important Religious Movements

From these periods of literary endeavour and of philosophy, there came three important religious developments. Two of these developments arose from religious reformers, who sought to find a way to break the power of *karma*.

(a) *Jainism*

The first was Vardhamana Mahavira, who believed that the path lay through abstinences and inactivity. Mahavira, a monk, was probably born about 569 B.C., and his followers form the Jain community. This community numbers today about one million and a quarter. Its members form an inner circle of strict persons (many of whom are merchants and bankers), who are born of the Brahmin caste. They are very concerned to do no harm to any living thing, so they strain their drinks to avoid swallowing any organism and filter their breath through a respirator. They worship a group of deities, known as the *Tirthankaras*, who are heroic and enlightened individuals who have already achieved blessedness. These *Tirthankaras* form a kind of corporate deity but are not responsive to human need, and in fact are subject also to re-birth in another life.

(b) *Buddhism*

The second great reformer, who also came from the same Kshatriya or warrior caste and was concerned to break the power of *karma*, was Gautama Buddha. Siddhartha Gautama was born, about the year 560 B.C., into a family of noble lineage, who lived at Kapilavastu, a city in the north-east of India, close to the frontier with Nepal. He sought to find peace at heart by various techniques, such as yoga, but was not successful. At last, when he was thirty-five years old, while he was sitting cross-legged beneath a pipul or bo-tree, he received the 'enlightenment' which he sought. Henceforth he was known as 'the Buddha' or 'the Enlightened One'. He set out as a teacher to give the light that had come to him, namely, that life's sorrows arise out of desire. He produced a 'Noble Eight-fold Path' to help men to eliminate desire and to enable them to attain 'Nirvana'.

As he rejected the idea of a Supreme Being, so it was

needful to provide a 'path' for men to find their own salvation. To this end, he rejected the paths of knowledge and asceticism but sought by meditation and moral duty to point the way to freedom. It was a practical path, avoiding extremes, yet it did not give much place to individuality. The teaching was accepted only slowly, as it gave no place to sacrificial practices which were popular. In fact, in time, Hinduism found this faith of Buddhism to be a challenge to older beliefs. There were also sharp divisions between different groups with Buddhism. These came to a head at the Council of Patna (*c.* 270–240 B.C.), after which two forms of Buddhism developed. The majority or the 'orthodox' developed into the 'Hinayana or Theravada Buddhism', which grew extensively in Burma, Ceylon and Siam. It is often called Southern Buddhism.

The minority group, known as Mahayana or Northern Buddhism, expanded in the northern lands, including China, Korea and Japan. The overthrow of the dynasty of King Asoka in India, where he had patronised the Buddha's teaching and had called the Council of Patna, resulted in the return to power of the Brahmins and their teaching. This caused the Buddhists to leave their home country of India and seek to live their way of life elsewhere. In this way, Buddhism came to be widely accepted in the East.

Theravada Buddhism stresses the place of the 'Dharma' (or law), and the 'Sangha' (or Order of Monks), whose lives are set apart to seek enlightenment, abstaining from many pleasures. In Burma, many children for a short period spend some time serving in a Buddhist monastery. There was held a Great Buddhist Council in Rangoon in 1956. This branch of Buddhism believes that the selfhood of a person is an illusion and has no continuance after death.

It is estimated that there are about 100,000 Buddhist priests in Burma in a population of some 18 million.

Mahayana Buddhism has two important features which are lacking in the Southern form, namely, the conception of a Buddha-spirit, which is incarnate in the *bodhisattvas* (saints) and the thought that the human spirit is a continuant. The idea of the bodhisattvas has been mentioned in connection with Buddhism in China. The Buddha-spirit (*Dharmakaya*) is found in these 'saints', who, in their love and compassion for their fellows, do not go to the place of bliss but return to spread enlightenment to those on earth. This Buddha-spirit finds expression in a number of saviour-gods, of whom O-mi-t'o-fu (*Amitabha*), Mi-lei-fo (*Maitreya*), Kuan Yin (*Avalokitesvara*) and Pi-lu-fo (*Vairocana*) are the most prominent. Images of these gods are prominent and precious for the illiterate.

The idea of the human soul as a continuant means that, instead of *karma* (a continuation in some form of existence which may take a higher or lower form), the human soul may pass through a number of heavens or hells to attain a final condition of individual bliss. The classic document of this Mahayana Buddhism is called the *Lotus Sutra* or *The Lotus of the True Law*, which is acknowledged by the twelve main Buddhist groups of Japan, as well as being widely recognised in China and Korea.

(c) *The Bhakti Saints*

The third important movement is the development of the idea of the *Bhakti*, which is an attempt to seek union between a universal Lord (*Isvara*) and the soul, in an intimate personal relationship. It is in fact a fervent personal religion, seeking to find salvation in a trusting devotion to a personal deity by the loving soul which longs for union with a divine lover. This became prominent in India, after the time of Ramanuja, who died in 1250 B.C. There have been a number of Bhakti saints and writers in later centuries.

This longing for union gave great popularity also to some great Indian epics, namely, the *Mahabharata* and the *Ramayana*, which describe the human experiences of the god Vishnu, who is believed in these epics to have become incarnate for the sake of humanity. In the case of the *Mahabharata*, Vishnu is seen in the person of Krishna, a charioteer, who exhorts his princely master (Arjuna) in a series of discourses; and in the *Ramayana*, in the person of Rama or Ram, the hero king. Vishnu is a good god and is one of the Hindu Triad, of which the other two are Brahma and Shiva. Brahma fell into the background and Shiva is a god of destruction, in contrast to the good activities of Vishnu. Vishnu and Shiva represent the kind and the harsh faces of Nature, in creation and destruction.

Since the end of the fifteenth century, there has been an increasing European influence, which has brought, in particular, the beliefs of Christian missionaries, whose activity in educational circles has had profound effect. Such activity has, however, aroused some Indian leaders to seek to rekindle the fire of Hinduism. Thus, Dayanand Sarasvati (1824–83) founded in 1875 an association which is called the *Arya Samaj*, in an attempt to revive Vedic religion. Some Indian leaders have tried to bring some measure of Christianity into Hinduism, as Ram Mohan Roy (1772–1833), who founded a reformed Hindu sect, which is called the Brahma Samaj. The Mahatma Gandhi was strongly influenced by Christian beliefs although he remained a Hindu. The Indian writers, Tagore and Radha-krishnan, are also loyal to Hinduism but not to the older forms of conservative belief.

It is probably true of most major religions that they are both a cultural area and a religion. Hinduism is a cultural area, which covers a great diversity of behaviour and beliefs. To this cultural area, most Indians belong. Yet within this area, there are also beliefs which are more particularly religious (rites and sacred objects, a religious community and various observances). Many Indians may not follow these beliefs, rites and ceremonies of Hinduism as a religion, but they are still loyal to the larger cultural area of Indian thought and practice. The same can be claimed with regard to Islam. It is a large cultural area, which has Arabic as its sacred language and is centered on certain generally acknowledged practices (especially the sacred formula: 'There is one God and Muhammad is his prophet'). Yet in the wide area of Islam, from the African coast to the lands of South-East Asia, there are wide variations of faith, practice and local observance.

3. Religious Practice

In India today, there are a great number of temples, and religious services are often very elaborate. These require a trained priesthood who use ancient rituals and prayers to worship the great number of gods, although Vishnu and Shiva have risen to such prominence that they stand out from the rest. On the other hand, there are many Hindus who are dissatisfied with popular beliefs and have evolved elaborate philosophies which have developed from another group of sacred books, the *Upanishads*, which were written

about 500 B.C. Some of their beliefs and practices are very
ancient, especially the cult of the cow, which Mahatma
Gandhi believed was the one religious value held in common
by the entire Hindu world. The cow is a sacred object for
the Hindus and they abstain from eating it. In this matter,
they act in contrast to the beef-eating and non-pork-
eating Muslims and Jews.

The middle-class Hindu family has its own household
gods, to which offerings of grain or flowers are made daily.
For special occasions, such as a marriage, a particular
Brahmin priest will visit the home. There are traditional
ties between particular families and Brahmin families,
which continue through the generations. It is the duty of a
group of families to keep the Brahmin priest, who carries
out services for them. There are also a number of customary
practices, which include an early morning bath, a period of
meditation, abstinences from food at certain periods,
vegetarianism and abstinence from wine. When Indians
come to this country, they try to continue some of these
practices, but their tolerance inclines them to accept the
customs they find, unless they have had a very strict
upbringing.

4. Adaptation with Immigration

The close-knit pattern of the extended family group in
many Eastern countries is missed when members from such
families leave home and come to the West, where the family
group is often much smaller. The Indian or Pakistani who
comes to England misses the wider circle of the family, to
whom he can turn for advice and help. His neighbours in
England are not interested in him or his affairs but, in fact,

are often hostile to him as a 'foreigner'. This hurts his pride in that he has been a Commonwealth citizen from birth, and has taken pride in his loyalty to the Crown and Great Britain. He dislikes any patronising attitude towards him, which is shown in various ways. He often has to accept a lower-paid job, though his intelligence is worthy of a far better one. He may be invited to visit the home of some English person but when he accepts, he does not 'feel' as welcome as he had hoped and is seldom invited a second time.

On the other hand, many Indians suffer considerable disillusionment when they come to England. Their 'image' of the Westerner or the Britisher is that of an educated and well-fed person, similar to those whom they have met in India. But when they reach these shores, they are soon aware of economic rivalries, jealousies and conflicts, which indicate that educational opportunities have not made such great changes in the West, nor has Christianity the hold over the people that many of them had been led to believe. When the Indian middle-class person takes, in England, a 'lower-class' job, he is sometimes regarded as a snob by his work-mates, who 'take the mickey out of him'. If such a person is not fully accepted in his work-place among his work-mates and is not invited to their homes, then it is difficult for him to find his place as a fully accepted member of society.

This reveals a lack of communication between the older society and the newcomer. It is in the interest of all to find channels of social communication and understanding, which will help to integrate older and new units of society. Some of those from overseas, who wish to share our national heritage, have entered the churches to share in worship.

This also remains aloof for them. They do not meet people on a personal level. There are few clubs where they can meet the local 'native population' and with regard to the public houses, they have their own scruples about drinking alcohol and often meet hostility or prejudice there.

This lack of suitable means of social communication leads many to a sense of bitterness against the Western community. They wish to have the scientific knowledge and technical skills of the West, but they miss the ties of kinship and friendship which previously enabled them to feel that they 'belonged' to a community. Moreover, as they look around them in London, Birmingham and other large cities, where many of them go to find work, they are puzzled, if not angered, by the lack of respect towards the elderly and the neglect of the aged, which (for the Indian) denies the recognised duty of the son who has to care for his parents as a continuing debt of gratitude. It is evident that, on the part of one coming from the East as well as the one from the West, there is the common need for an understanding of the differences of each other's cultures. Such an understanding is made the more difficult, when those from overseas come in great numbers—too great to be easily absorbed into the existing neighbourhood relationships. Nevertheless, the stability as well as the serenity of the neighbourhood depends on the ability of the community to make room for the older residents and newcomers alike.

Summary

The variety of religious expression in India may well prove to be one of her outstanding contributions to human culture as a whole. The cultural differences in different parts of India are very wide, with historical and geographical roots, both of which affect man's outlook on the world and on his fellow creatures. It is, however, out of the wealth of material in his search for Reality, that the Indian can offer his varying types of solution to man's quest of faith.

On the one hand, there are a very large number of divine beings, who range from spirits of an animist type to the great god Vishnu, who becomes incarnate to serve as the helper of mankind. On the other hand, the passionate search for unity or *Advaita* (non-duality) has carried men's philosophical flights into new realms. It is to be expected that many thinkers in the West will find that to reach the heights and plumb the depths of the thought of Sankara and other Indian philosophers will open new dimensions to human thought. It is the wide panoramic conspectus of viewpoint that will appeal to a more universal culture, open to light from the East and from the West.

Nevertheless, the sense of illusion (*maya*) which pervades much of Indian thought will also serve to limit the appeal in many Western minds, which have been accustomed to think in terms of the purposeful activity of man in a creation in which he can co-operate with forces responsive to his activity. To posit Mind behind creation is a link, which possibly the West can contribute to the wealth of exploration, made through so many generations by Indian thinkers. Their mysticism and philosophy will without doubt appeal to many Western minds, who are unsatisfied by the secularist and materialist culture of a mechanistic age.

IV

CHINA'S ANCIENT CULTS

1. Introduction

When a Chinese family goes away from its home village to live somewhere else, there are recognised ways in which the family ties are retained with the old home. The Ancient Classics have acted as guiding lines in family and in public practice. The duties of piety towards the old home remain very strong. There is, for example, the necessity to send a portion of one's earnings to one's ageing parents as an expression of loyalty. The parents may not spend it wisely and the son or daughter may well be in serious need of the money, nevertheless the overseas son or daughter (who is dutiful) will make every effort to fulfil this obligation however hard it may be for them. Similarly, it is recognised that it is a duty to return home from time to time, to renew permission to be away and to report to the elder members of the family about the wellbeing of one's own family. An able middle-aged Chinese scholar who was invited to lecture as a Visiting Professor in the Universtity of New York admitted to me his regret that, due to political conditions, he had been unable to return to his mother (in the home village) to ask her permission to go abroad. Such family loyalty and solidarity has stood many tests.

It is not therefore a matter for surprise that cults which express this family loyalty still have their place in the family home. Many Chinese families who come to Britain have been connected with the Christian Church and so their observance of traditional practices, especially in the religious sphere, may be slight (and sometimes very slight). But it is to the more traditional type of family that this chapter has to give attention. This type of family brings its objects of worship with it and endeavours to uphold the standards and values of their culture.

The most familiar objects are those which are found in the main living room, where on a shelf there are placed a small censer (in which are sticks of incense), a tablet of one's ancestors and figures of gods, which are believed to bring success to the family. The tablet is a link with the past and is only really evident when one or two generations have died. These generations are the direct links with the older generations of the family. With their passing, their successors wish to remember the heritage from which they have come, so the tablet is a reminder of the long past of their people. This is of greater value than ever when it is more difficult to return to the mainland where the old home lies.

On the other hand, it has to be recognised that many overseas Chinese have thrown over many older practices, some because they just do not bother and others from a conscious desire to follow new ways, especially those who wish to pursue a Marxist path or a Maoist path. It is noteworthy, however, that Mao's thoughts often reflect the older Chinese tradition which helps to give them acceptance among the common people. Among Chinese families in Western countries, there are many who wish to act similarly to Western families and so there is less willingness to keep to tradition which lacks public opinion and support.

Nevertheless, there are figures of gods, which are found in their homes. An important figure is that of Kuan Yin, the Buddhist Goddess of Mercy, who gives children and is the patron saint of sailors. She is a Saviour-goddess, who carries those who worship her to the Isles of the Blessed. In China, she has universal acclaim as the giver of sons, and in the homes of the people she has a prominent place. The affection and adoration she receives does not cease when the family moves to a new country, where she takes her place among the precious family treasures. Kuan Yin has her place also as a craft goddess; dressed in white garments, she is the patroness of the cutters and polishers of jade.

All the various crafts have their particular craft gods and goddesses. Thus, there is the patron-god of carpenters, masons, varnishers and workers in stone, called Lu Pan, who is identified with an able craftsman of that name of the kingdom of Lu, in Shantung, and who was born in 506 B.C. From a Western point of view, the patron of clock-makers is interesting, as he is Li Ma-tu, who is none other than the famous Jesuit missionary, P. Matteo Ricci (1552-1610), who had ability as an astronomer, a mathematician and a clock-maker. Such craftsmen of guilds do not travel far to the West but students and men of commerce are more frequent. Among students, the traditional figure of respect is the god of literature, Wen-ch'ang, who is depicted in academic costume, with a ceremonial hat and a solemn inexpressive face. He is sometimes accompanied by two assistants, who are the god of literary examinations and the god of good fortune.

Among the men of commerce, the popular figure is the god of wealth, Ts'ai-shen, who has a prominent place in many homes as a giver of prosperity. In the West, while he may not be worshipped, yet a picture of him, or an image, may be found as part of the decoration of the living room. He may not receive much attention, though, on special occasions, perhaps before some business deal, a small stick of incense may be burned before him in respect. Such small acts as a prayer or bowings may form the only outward signs of worship, yet he holds a place in the hearts of many in their desire for wealth. He is particularly prominent in the shops of goldsmiths and in the homes of shopkeepers generally. The Chinese in the West are most frequently found in laundries and in restaurants.

Apart from these figures of patron-gods, there are a great number of characters, which are deemed to be highly efficacious in bringing good fortune. Such characters are those who indicate 'Heaven' (*T'ien*), 'Happiness' (*Fu*), 'Public Office' (*Lu*) and 'Long Life' (*Shou*). These are only common instances of such characters which have a wide and common use in many Chinese homes. They are displayed on pictures, scrolls and carvings. It is regarded as a token of bliss and security to have such tokens of well-being around the house or the shop as the case may be. The same characters are used for amulets and brooches and other ornaments. In Chinese homes, these same characters are often painted over the door as a symbol of good fortune as you enter the room.

In China itself, there is a great belief in the influence of the constellations and in the stars, which are believed to affect one's fate. Therefore, the casting of horoscopes is frequently found, although such practices may well be discredited under the Maoist regime. Formerly, an official calendar was issued to show the 'permitted' days for various actions, whether taking out the baby, entering upon a business contract and celebrating a marriage, and the 'non-permitted' days, when it was dangerous to undertake a new enterprise, according to the stellar positions, the sacred festivals and other influences. While the Chinese in Western homes may hold less firmly to such beliefs, it is to be expected that they are still greatly influenced by horoscopes. It has to be admitted that the magazines and newspapers of the so-called 'Christian West' still follow the practice of publishing horoscopes after long centuries of Christian teaching, so it is hardly reasonable to expect the Chinese, who have practised such casting of horoscopes for thousands of years, to abandon the practice very easily.

2. Religious Practices

The religious practices in the Chinese home mainly stem from the three Ways or Religions of China. These three Ways are Confucianism, Taoism and Buddhism.

(a) *Confucianism*

Confucianism is an ancient medley of beliefs, including elements of Nature worship, a deep respect (in many cases amounting to worship) for the ancestors and a code of moral law. This Way has been influential in China for many hundreds of years. *The Books of the Five Classics* (*The Book of History; Book of Odes; Book of Changes; Book of Rites* and the *Spring and Autumn Annals*) have served as models for the intellectual and governing classes of China. Mao Tse-Tung acknowledges his debt to the Confucian tradition, which is also a recognition that to be a true Chinese one needs to be within this tradition. Even those who deny the religious aspects of Confucianism recognise the importance of the moral training and teaching of Confucius and his disciples, especially of Mencius.

(b) *Taoism*

Taoism has supplied the elements of mystery, romance and colour to off-set the stern moral codes of Confucianism. It is claimed that the father of Taoism is Lao-Tzu (*c.* 604 B.C.), an older contemporary of Confucius, and a teacher, to whom is attributed the sacred work, known as the *Tao-teh-ching*, which in its present form probably dates from the second century B.C. Taoism has incorporated within itself a floating mass of folk-lore and mythology from early times. It has deified Lao-Tzu and a great number of legendary and real figures in Chinese history. It has also made gods of many natural forces, particularly of mountains. Such beliefs have been easy to accept for those who have been animist or believers in various kinds of spirits. In Taoism there is a wide use of amulets and charms for sickness and for practically every sort of occasion.

There is also in Taoism the appeal of the 'natural', the desire to be set free from conflict and struggle, which in other religions is known as 'quietism'. The Taoist mystic seeks that communion with Nature, that inner harmony— such as William Wordsworth expresses in his *Lines composed a few miles above Tintern Abbey*, as he learned

> To look on nature, . . . hearing oftentimes
> The still, sad music of humanity
> . . . . a sense sublime
> Of something far more deeply interfused . . .
> A motion and a spirit, that impels
> All thinking things, all objects of all thought,
> And rolls through all things. . . .

While the Confucian scholar stressed action and moral decision, the Taoist priest sought to be detached from affairs. The Confucianist stressed the duties in this life towards the State, the family and one's friends; the Taoist sought to penetrate into the mysteries—to seek the Golden Isles and to turn (by alchemy) ordinary metals into gold. Many of the Chinese secret societies have been associated with Taoism, which blessed charms which (so it was believed) could protect the owner. Such charms it was hoped would turn back a bullet upon the marksman and shield the believer from danger. There is a Taoist Pope in China and he is a descendant from a certain Chang Tao Ling, who is said to have lived in the first Christian century. An important Taoist god is known as the Pearly Emperor (Yu Huang) and he is depicted in many pictures and appears in many popular stories.

(c) *Mahayana Buddhism*

The third Way is that of Mahayana or Northern Buddhism, which entered China from India about A.D. 61. This faith acknowledged the fine ethical elements of the native faiths, especially in Confucianism, and has been tolerant towards other faiths. But Buddhism has brought in many elements which were lacking in the earlier native faiths. These elements include definite beliefs about the future life and an elaborate philosophy which appealed to the intellectual Chinese. This philosophy was written down in an extensive literature which was gradually brought from India and was translated into Chinese. It proved a stimulating and fertile field for imaginative writing and has had wide repercussions in literature and in the arts generally.

On the other hand, for the ordinary people, who could not read and write, Buddhism also had a wide appeal. This has been due to its ornate ritual and its stories of a rich mystical life. The glories of the Seven Heavens and the terrors of Hell have been depicted in glowing terms to keep believers on the path of faith. In particular, the goddess Kuan Yin has proved to be an ardent object of adoration, particularly among women, who have little place in the worship of the native faiths. This goddess provided help at the beginning of life, when she is deemed to provide sons and preside over child-birth, as well as at the close of life, when she steers the believers to the Isles of Sakhavati or the Western Paradise on the 'Bark of Salvation'. She is regarded as the Saviour and Deliverer of all living beings. Thus, in the words of the American historian, Kenneth Latourette, 'Buddhism . . . ran counter to none of the fundamental beliefs and . . . offered to fill a void.' Thus it has filled a large place in the religious life of the Chinese, with monasteries and nunneries in all parts of China.

When death comes, it is frequently the Buddhist priest who is called in to take charge of the funeral ceremonies. Buddhist funerals are often very elaborate, since the deceased is believed to require many of the articles which he has used in this life. Such articles are provided by the family and friends in the form of paper imitations of the articles themselves, including such items as paper houses paper cars and bicycles, with an infinite variety of smaller gifts. Prayers are recited by the priest (or priests) and, according to the wealth of the family, a great number of friends join the procession to the family grave and later share in a feast in the family home. It is not simply an individual matter. The family honour is at stake in providing adequately for the guests and so a great amount of money is often spent on such provision. The burial place is chosen with great care to ensure that the 'wind and water' (*feng-shui*) influences are correct. These influences are believed to be the natural spirits of the universe, harmony with whom will enable the deceased to rest in peace.

With the coming of Buddhism, the use of temples and ornate rituals in a more public setting became more widely adopted. The images of the Buddha in various forms were displayed in temples to which those in need went for help in cases of sickness, to secure decisions by means of divination, to make petitions (e.g. for sons) and to meditate on the sacred writings there. The measure of literacy among the Buddhist priests greatly differs in various temples and monasteries. Some priests visit the homes of the believers to teach them to recite the sacred writings and to provide a degree of literacy. Taoist and Confucian shrines were built in imitation of the Buddhist shrines, and so temples have become a widespread and popular feature in the Chinese countryside.

An important aspect of Northern Buddhism is the belief in *bodhisattvas*, that is, in those human beings who are regarded as saints. These beings are considered to be those who, out of compassion and love for their fellows, refrain from attaining Nirvana (the goal of full enlightenment), so that they may be able to spread the saving knowledge of the Way among mankind. Thus, beneficent individuals, who have shown compassion and help to their fellows in their lifetime, continue to be respected and honoured as 'saints' after their death. In country towns, the images of former benefactors (male and female) are paraded through the streets on their festival days (normally the birth or death day of the person concerned). There is often much excitement, with fire-crackers and the burning of sticks of incense, with special prayers to these benefactors, so that they will continue to be a beneficent influence in the community.

These images have provided objects of worship, particularly for those who are unable to read, in Buddhism, which, in its original form, does not seem to believe in a personal deity. In the form of Buddhism which is found in China, Gautama Buddha himself is also deified and there is a belief in salvation as a way of faith in Gautama himself and by the repetition of the names of his saints (*bodhisattvas*). The personal Buddha as the supreme object of worship is seen in the classic document, known as the *Lotus Sutra*, in which the glorified and transcendent Gautama is surrounded by thousands of gods and bodhisattvas. This Sutra has great fame in the Far East and is acknowledged by all the twelve main Buddhist denominations in Japan. It is perhaps in the vivid portrayals of heaven and hell that this form of Buddhism has secured the firmest hold on the popular imagination, since it sets before the devotee the hope of personal immortality.

These Three Ways of Religion have received most attention in most text-books on Chinese Religion. These Ways have the most elaborate rites and rituals and are most evident, yet they only express in part the religious practices of the Chinese people. An ancient Chinese Classic, entitled *The Book of Rites*, claims that 'the rites and ceremonies do not go down to the common people' but, without doubt, the ordinary Chinese family has its religious forms and ceremonies. In fact, it is clear that the whole of the life of the Chinese family is interpenetrated by religion.

(d) *Popular Religion*

This religion of the common people is seen to be a strange mixture, which combines elements taken from the three Ways already described, yet forming together a 'Way', which now has a distinctness of its own. The form that is taken by this popular religion may be seen from its various aspects. These include the gods of the home; the sacred significance of family events; the use of the Chinese Almanac and divination; the place of religious festivals and of popular gods—forming together a composite picture of family worship which may be found in homes throughout China. There are wide varieties from home to home and province to province, especially with the powerful impact of Marxist and Maoist thought, yet it is to be expected that in many homes, the older practices will take a long time to be replaced while the family units are able to preserve their identity and loyalties. The gods of the house are assigned duties in every room, so that there are the door-gods, the gods of the bedroom, of the cess-pool and the well, as well as the god of the kitchen. This last god (of the kitchen) has had particular significance as a guardian and censor of family morals and behaviour, as he is considered to be most intimately connected with informal family practice.

As the women spend much time in the kitchen, this god has been thought to know most about their behaviour. In the guest room, the host or hostess may be very polite but in the kitchen, he or she will express their true feelings, which are known to the kitchen god. Therefore, when (at the close of the Chinese year) this god went to report to the Jade Emperor on the twenty-fourth day of the twelfth month, it was the practice to place a meal before his image—

including melons, a wheaten cake of red beans, candied fruit, a special white sugared sticky rice and a bowl of sweet wine. Later, the mouth of the god's image was smeared with syrup to ensure a good report. When the god was believed to be on his journey, firecrackers were lighted as an expression of relief and devotion.

As among all peoples, the changing stages in human life need to be socially recognised, so the ceremonies (*rites de passage*) have been carefully observed in the various family events. From the child's birth (as well as previous to it), there has to be great care to take no action which might be inauspicious or unlucky. The suitable colours, charms, times and occasions have to be observed, to ensure that the child will pass the various barriers which threaten the young life. In days when modern medical science was unknown, there were many killer diseases. The illnesses of children became personified as spirits which threatened the child's life and as barriers, which numbered thirty in Taoist practice. As each barrier was reached, so suitable safeguards had to be taken. These thirty dangerous barriers extended from birth until the age of sixteen years and their peril for the child depended on the month, day and hour of the birth of the child. The fortune-teller was believed to be able to inform the parents how to overcome the demons which guarded these dangerous barriers. At the end of the first year of life, the demon who guarded that barrier was believed to have no further power.

3. Modern Adaptation

The continuation of these practices will widely differ from home to home, especially outside China. In some cases, these practices are regarded as part of Chinese tradition and therefore they are carried out as an expression of loyalty to China, an act of patriotism such as we display when we stand for the national anthem. But there is little doubt that scientific ways of thought will undermine their faith in amulets and horoscopes and in nature spirits. The attitude of fatalism towards sickness and disease will be replaced by a determined attempt to find the causes of disease. Whereas in the past, a disease was attributed to a goddess of malaria or smallpox, now the material and environmental causes will be sought to overcome these scourges. For example, in Hankow (Central China), strenuous efforts have been made to prevent the breeding of the mosquitoes which act as carriers of malaria. Water-butts and open water pits, where such insects settle, have been enclosed to prevent the spread of a sickness which has reduced the abilities of so many Chinese for a long period. Similarly, the use and distribution of modern drugs, together with more health education, will reduce the amount of illness, which, in the past, has been taken to be inevitable.

At the same time, the Buddhist and Taoist priests have been made to spend some time on manual tasks (and even in factories), instead of remaining in the monasteries. Therefore, the religious life which is changing inside China will strongly influence the practices of those who have come from China and now live in the Western countries. It is not easy to establish the extent to which family worship is continued in the inner provinces of China but it is probable that many families will continue their age-long practices as long as they can—teaching the younger generations to carry on their traditions.

On the other hand, there will undoubtedly be a great change from earlier days. Many of the young people have been among the 'Red Guards', as teenagers who have travelled from the countryside or from upcountry towns to gather in the larger cities in mass rallies. The life of the great cities has been seen by thousands of young people who would never have travelled in this way, even ten years ago. Their outlook and their future will certainly be influenced considerably by the great movements in the population. It may be that the Chinese nation, which is so large, will come to realise itself as more people see more of their homeland. The roots in the countryside may come to have less significance as the requirements of factory life cause more people to be moved from the country to new urban centres, where the factories are established.

Industrialisation in China has not been extensive but as it expands and more industries and factories are set up, so more people will have to move from the land to new places. These moves will also have a profound effect upon the older religious beliefs as many of the gods are rooted in the land where the family has farmed for many generations. The need for a universal faith will become increasingly apparent. Buddhism and Taoism will endeavour to meet this need. The creed of Maoist-Marxist thought will also try to satisfy the need, but it is probable that a faith which reconciles China with other nations as well as meets the need of individual human lives will alone provide a 'Way' to a new harmony with Heaven and Earth. There are many earnest seekers after a true 'Way' in China and this is apparent from the many great thinkers who have been prominent in her history.

Summary

The religious quest in China is practical and seeks to find expressions to meet the needs of the whole nature of man.

The practical demands are seen in the devotion paid to the little earth deities, who preside over the plots of land and are responsible for fertility. It is quite clear that responsibility can be placed at the door of this or that deity when supplies are not forthcoming. The offices and duties of the various gods are the reflection of a people, whose bureaucratic society has been so ordered for hundreds of years.

Yet, such local deities can only provide certain kinds of help. The greater gods are needed to control the constellations and the whole order of Nature. The search for harmony has stimulated the thinkers of many schools, whose imaginative thought has found expression in the Taoist writings, with their flights of fancy, their passion for charms and their 'feeling' for Nature. Taoism could only fill part of the gap, which Buddhism was able to bridge by the wealth of intellectual scholarship, ornate ceremonial and reassurance of a blessed immortality. The plain duties of the household were meanwhile the responsibility of the Confucian literati, who spelled out the ways in which harmony was to be found in the ordering of society.

The practicality of much Communist thought will appeal to the same sentiments in present-day China. The emotional and intellectual demands remain, however, and it will be interesting to discover the way, in which these demands will be met. Much of the older religious mythology will undoubtedly remain as fairy-tale fancy to delight the imagination but the deeper questions on the true nature of man, the ultimate destiny of society and of creation need to find more searching answers than have yet been given.

V

THE WAY OF JAPAN

1. Introduction

The religious life of Japan is made up of a number of elements, of which the main ones are Shinto, Buddhism and Confucianism, of which Shinto alone is indigenous. The fact that Buddhism and Confucianism have gained many followers in Japan reveals that the indigenous belief lacked certain factors and also that Japan has been open to the influences from the mainland even though, at times, the Government has tried to prevent the invasion of ideas from outside the islands.

From a very early period in her history, a Nature mythology has served as a basis of religious belief. Such mythology explains the origin of things as a process of growth, which makes little distinction between gods and Nature. Creation is explained as the result of spontaneity, then by procreation or by magical emanation (for example, the Sun-goddess *Amatersu* was born from the left eye of the male god named *Izanagi*). The traditional history of Japan is found in early records, such as the *Kojiki* (Chronicles of Ancient Events': *c.* A.D. 712—the oldest extant Japanese historical record) and the *Nihongi* ('Chronicles of Japan'—which was compiled from earlier documents about the year A.D. 720). Long before this time, Chinese and Indian influences had begun to modify the indigenous religion

54

from a period early in the Christian era, when the introduction of writing from the mainland also brought Chinese literature, which contained Confucian and Buddhist doctrines.

2. Religious Belief and Practice

(a) *Shinto*

In the *Nihongi*, there first appears the term 'Shinto' (from the Chinese 'Shen' 'Tao'—'The Way of the Gods'). This term covers a wide range of deities, which were originally believed to have sprung from a void. According to their tradition, there were a succession of deities, first of all three and then a number of pairs of deities until there arose *Izanagi* (male) and *Izanami* (female), with which gods the main cosmogony begins.

The two gods were instructed by the heavenly deities to create and consolidate the drifting land, so they cast their jewelled spears into the waves and fixed an island. By their embrace, these gods are believed to have given birth to the various islands of Japan and to the various nature deities including the springs, the trees, the mountains and all living things.

The last child of the goddess Izamami was none other than *Ho-musubi* (the sun's heat), who not only gives warmth but also, in excess, causes destruction. (This is one manifestation of the universal practice of the worship of the sun, which, in some places, like Mexico, was exceedingly cruel and demanded innumerable human sacrifices.) This last child of Izanami destroyed his mother and caused the wrath of his father, who in turn destroyed him. The male god Izanagi went into the underworld in search of his wife and then speedily returned and washed in the sea, in which he brought forth more deities. From his left eye sprang *Amaterasu* (the Sun-goddess) and from his right eye the Moon-god, while from his nostrils sprang the Storm-god.

The Sun-goddess, *Amatersu Omi-kami*, also had her adventures. Her brother, *Susa-no-wo*, the storm-god, ill-treated her and she had perforce to hide in a cave, with the result that the world was filled with darkness. However, she was enticed out again by a mirror, which has become her sacred symbol and is the chief treasure of her ancient shrine at Ise, on the south coast. Every Shinto shrine has a mirror as her symbol. It is by her beneficence, shining in six directions on the earth, that all things prosper.

The importance of this goddess has been enhanced by the belief in her connection with the royal house. It is believed that the goddess became supreme among the gods and sent her grandson, Ninigi, to the earth to bring order. Ninigi is believed to be the progenitor of the imperial family, which rules by the authority of the gods. This belief has been an important factor in the strongly traditional (and at times isolated) life of the Japanese people. It made the acts of the Emperor as beyond question—since they came by divine authority.

As in the case of ancient Egypt, the authority of the ruling house lay in the ruler's solar descent and was not open to ethical considerations. It also followed from this close connection with the supreme goddess that Japan was believe to be superior to other nations as its ruler had this peculiar and special authority by his divine lineage. It is his ancestry that has been stressed, but he has been regarded as *akitsu-kami* (manifest or incarnate deity). (In his New Year message, on January 1st, 1946, the Emperor renounced his divinity but belief in his sacred person has been a powerful element in the national scene.)

The term *kami* is used widely to express superhuman power (as in Polynesia the term *mana* is used). It is used to signify the deities of heaven and earth, the spirits of the shrines, peculiar-shaped natural objects (such as mountains, animals and plants) or, in fact, any particularly mysterious object or person, including thunder, dragons, dwarfs and other strange phenomena. As all things have emanated from a very primitive state, wherein the divine is manifest in nature as in man, so there has arisen a form of nature-worship which has strong materialistic tendencies. The divine is not regarded as a superior transcendent principle but rather all nature is regarded as divine. In consequence, Shintoism has been strongly materialistic and also has been man-centred, without any clear meaning or purpose in creation. It may be claimed, however, that *kami* is potentially personal or finds itself often associated with shrines and personal objects within them.

Shintoism has been assisted by its close connection with patriotic feeling and loyalty towards the ruling house. In fact, from 1870 until 1939, there was very restrictive legislation to permit only those religious groups which were compatible with the doctrines of State Shinto. In 1954 General McArthur disestablished State Shinto and gave full permission for freedom of worship. In 1945 there were some forty-three groups recognised by the authorities (viz., 13 sects of Shinto, 28 of Buddhism and 2 of Christianity). However, with the freedom of worship, there has been a rapid expansion of sects and new cults, so that by 1951 there were 720, which included 258 sects of Shinto, 260 of Buddhism, 46 of Christianity and 156 'others'. Many of these were fraudulent and made money out of the credulity of illiterate people, so that a weeding-out process had to take place. This has resulted in a lower total of officially recognised cults, which in 1962 numbered 171.

(b) *Buddhism*

The primitive indigenous religion of Japan has been greatly modified by Buddhism, which has acted as a powerful spiritual force to promote literature, art, education, philosophy and a kinder approach to life (including the care of the sick and of animals). It was introduced into Japan from Korea, when a king of a south-western kingdom sought help from Japan in A.D. 552. Shinto acted as a responsive ally to tolerant Buddhism, so that the latter spread under the patronage of Prince Regent Shotoku (A.D. 592–621). The Hinayana sects (*Kusha*, *Jo-Jitsu* and *Sanson*) which proclaimed nihility and 'emptiness' proved to have little appeal for the vigorous Japanese and became extinct. It was the Mahayana sects (*Jodo* and *Shin-shu*) which prevailed, especially as these sects (known as 'Pure Land' sects) proclaimed the Mahayana doctrine of 'salvation by faith' in the work of *Amida Buddha*.

It was inevitable that there should be a considerable amount of mixing of faiths or syncretism, which is seen as early as A.D. 805, when the *Tendai* priests brought from China an idealistic eclectic system, which was based on the teaching of the *Saddharma Pundarikasutra* or 'The Lotus of the True Law'. In this religious system, all the Buddhas are considered to be ultimately one true Reality. In fact, all the manifold plurality of forms are regarded as manifestations of the ultimate Reality but the indigenous and native *kami* are given their place within this unity as manifest Buddhas. The Shinto pantheism is given an interpretation which will fit in with Buddhist conceptions of the universe.

Among the sects of Buddhism, three main methods of salvation emerged, namely, *Shodomin* (self-help), *Jadomin* (the help of another) and *dhydna* (meditation). In the Jodo sects, salvation is ascribed to the work of Amida Buddha, whose help is available to all, irrespective of social class and education.

In the Pure Land sects, there is not only the conception of a personal Saviour but also the hope of a Western Paradise, which has a prominent place in Mahayana Buddhism. There has been a great accumulation of sects, which have broken off from one another—as one refinement after another has taken place in the teachings of successive 'founders' and 'foundresses' of sects. A consideration of the causes for so many of the present sects will be deferred to a later point in this chapter. An example of this refinement is seen in that after the Pure Land Sect (*Jodo*), there came the 'True Pure Land Sect' (*Shin*). Another important group of sects are the *Zen* (Meditation) Sects, which have their devotees, seeking by mystic and quietistic paths the way to peace. The incessant repetition of the sacred name of a deity (such as Amida Buddha) is believed to secure merit and to provide the help required to meet life's daily battles.

(c) *Confucianism*

Less apparent, but still important, has been the influence of Confucianism in Japan. It has reinforced loyalty to the throne, strengthened filial piety and family relationships, and upheld benevolence and justice, while it has encouraged ancestor worship. The Confucian conception of the two principles of the universe, known as *Yin* and *Yang* (light and darkness, male and female), is seen in the dualistic expression of the *In* and *Yo* in Japan. In the seventeenth century, when the ruling class held Buddhism in disfavour, Neo-confucianism was encouraged and various teachers were supported and schools arose. However, it has been the warmer personal sects of Buddhism which have received greater favour, as these fill a gap which is left unfilled by the colder moralistic temper of the Confucian teaching.

3. Modern Developments

Reference has been made in the previous section to the rapid growth in the number of sects. These sects have a mixture of beliefs and practices, drawn from various religious sources (of the East and the West) and so are 'syncretistic', a prominent feature of Japanese religion. Some of these sects appear to be 'new', but their doctrines mainly follow familiar patterns of *minkan-shinko* (folk-beliefs), which were discouraged after 1870 as primitive ('pre-modern') and as in conflict with State Shinto. Some appear modern, as in the case of the Denshinkyo (now dissolved) which worshipped electricity and had Thomas Edison as one of its lesser deities. Another sect (the Kokusai Dai Nippon Fuso Shinjunkai) made its chief deity the late Dr. Frederick Starr of Chicago University.

Most of the sects worship Bodhisattvas and Shinto gods, which have been known for centuries. These gods provide mundane benefits, both here and hereafter, in return for worship. The central emphasis of many of these sects seems to serve to relieve the overwhelming sense of insecurity, anxiety and uncertainty about the future, whether in regard to family-trouble, money, illness, adolescence or other matters. The fact that there were comparatively few social services in Japan at the close of the war, together with the insecurity of post-war ordinary living, made life even more difficult to bear after political defeat and the collapse of a (believed) invincible creed. People sought a way of escape from *happo-fusagari* (eight directions blocked). For many people, the sects provide an organised and dedicated group experience and the offer of mundane benefits, which are lacking in the older traditional forms of religious life.

The characteristics of these sects may be briefly stated. They normally centre around a religious centre, such as the huge Tenrikyo headquarters near Nara and the impressive Soka Gakkai centre at Mount Fuji. Their doctrines are easy to understand and to follow and are mainly optimistic— 'religions of happiness', with festivals and fireworks. They claim to be able to establish the Kingdom of God on earth here and now, granting painless childbirth, present release from poverty, healing by faith and other benefits. Many of them stress the unity of religion and life as in the Kitamura Sayo with its emphasis on social work and in the Ittoen (Garden of Light), whose members once a week clean toilets in nearby towns. They all rely upon a strong leader or group of leaders, often with the assistance of an able organiser. The doctrines taught give the members a sense of dignity and importance, although they teach the relativity of all religions, except for Soka Gakkai which is strongly intolerant of other beliefs.

Among these characteristics, the role of the Founders and Foundresses is very significant. These leaders invite the transference of worry and anxiety and claim a direct revelation from God or Buddha. They speak with tongues and claim to lead their followers to Paradise. There are similar patterns in the early life of these Founders—they are nearly always from poor low-class families (peasants and small shopkeepers); they usually have bitter early tribulations—with harsh treatment from mothers-in-law or masters or fathers, which is followed by serious illness, from which there is a miraculous recovery, with trances and divine deliverances. The believers claim that they have received great help from the overwhelmingly powerful personality of the Founder or Foundress, who has powers which may be called 'shamanic' such as clairvoyance, weather-power and power over demon possession.

An interesting example is the sect known as the Dancing Religion (Odoru Shukyo), which has its base at Tabusi, in the West of Japan (some two hours' train journey from Hiroshima). There lives the Foundress—a peasant woman of 68 years of age, friendly and hospitable—whose original name is Katamara Sayo. (She is known by her followers as *Ogamisama* (great goddess) and they worship her as divine.) She claims that she is third in line of true teachers after Buddha and Christ—she also claims that Buddhism and Christianity are dead and in some aspects, she is intolerant of other faiths. In her teaching, there is evidence of elements of both Buddhist and Christian origin. The teaching is simple and is stimulated by the 'Self-less Dance' (*Muga-ni-mai*), which awakens a warm emotional state of corporate pleasure. The Foundress has nominated her grand-daughter to be her successor. In other sects, the mantle of leadership may fall, on the founder's death, on his wife or son or sometimes just peter out. Some groups are efficiently organised and can carry on without such a powerful figurehead, as in the case of the Soka Gakkai, although an efficient organiser normally initiates the movement.

The sect of the Soka Gakkai has some particularly interesting aspects as it has been organised on the pattern of a high-powered highly organised business enterprise of the twentieth century. It began as a lay group, in 1930, under Makiguchi Tsunesaburo, a former Tokyo elementary school principal, who held a training course on the teachings of Nichiren, who founded a Buddhist sect, known as Nichiren Sect, in the thirteenth century. A lay association was formed as a 'scholarly association for the increase of values' (Soka Gakkai). This became associated closely with the Nichiren Shoshu (the 'True Sect' of Nichiren), which was one of the thirty-six branches, which developed out of the original Nichiren teaching.

The monk Nichiren, who originally belonged to an older Buddhist sect (the Tendai sect), lived in tumultuous days in the thirteenth century, when there were threats from Mongol invasions and serious social unrest but also great expansion of Buddhist teaching. Nichiren emphasised the Lotus Sutra as the quintessence of Buddhist teaching. He was very intolerant of all other sects to which he attributed all the ills of his time. He wrote a *mandala* (or sacred manuscript), which extolled Japan's place in the world and also the importance of the teaching of the Buddha.

Makiguchi did not at first meet with much success, so that during the period from 1930 to 1937 the membership of the group only increased to sixty members, although Makiguchi had an able lieutenant in his director general, named Toda Josei. The fierce intolerance of this sect and the unwillingness of the adherents to worship the Sun-goddess brought the group under the displeasure of the authorities. A large number of the members of the sect were imprisoned in 1941 and remained there until the end of the war. Makiguchi died in prison in 1944 and it was left to Toda Josei to reconstitute the group when he came out of prison in 1945.

The freedom of worship and the disestablishment of State Shinto at the close of the war resulted in untrammelled religious activity, which has been called 'the rush hour of the gods'. By 1951, the group under the able leadership of Toda numbered five thousand members and had been given a military organisation as well as a missionary purpose. The missionary endeavour lies in the aim of each believer to convert three other persons each year by the method of *shakubuku* (breaking and subduing). This method, advocated by Nichiren in his intolerance of others' views, consists in refuting other religious beliefs and persuading others to accept the sect's teaching.

Many social factors have contributed to the success of Toda's work. Despite its gorgeous ceremonies and ritual, State Shinto has now been discredited and the Emperor's authority is no longer able to suppress religious groups. The post-war suffering, low wages and unemployment contributed to the appeal of this group, who claimed to provide the way to personal peace and prosperity. Unlike some of the sects, Toda and other leaders continued to lead frugal lives, and when Toda died in 1958 the leadership passed to a form of collective leadership under a board of directors, with a Secretary General.

Toda realised the value of a powerful military organisation and, in 1955, moved into the political field. It was, however, in the elections of 1959, that the most striking results were secured. All 76 of the Soka Gakkai candidates in the Tokyo area were elected to the 23 town assemblies and 261 of their 287 candidates throughout the nation were elected. Also, in 1959, all six Soka Gakkai candidates were elected to the Upper House, the House of Counsellors, as it is called. Since then, they have increased their seats to 25 and have begun to win seats in the Lower House of Representatives. They are now the third largest party in the Upper House. These seats have been won by the leaders allocating members to vote in particular constituencies as permitted under the new constitution of May 1947. This sect has also conflicted with trade union organisations, especially Tanro (the giant coal-miners' union) at Hokkaido, claiming by its teaching to settle strikes and prevent diseases, which has caused many miners to turn from the unions to Soka Gakkai.

The emphasis of the Soka Gakkai is to create a heaven on earth, to encourage belief in faith-healing and to proclaim that it has the answer to money and personal problems. In the light of its connection with the Nichiren sect, it resents that it is a new sect—since the sects are held in contempt by the Japanese intelligentsia. It is, however, in its militant organisation and its intolerance that it is most untypically Buddhist.

When a person is in need (money, sorrow, etc.), a Soka Gakkai member will come to provide assistance, material as well as spiritual, narrating his own experience and that of others in the sect. By the use of books and newspapers, required reading, the economic basis helped. Invitation to a group for a convert builds up until there is a fifteen-family unit (*kumi*), forming close-knit communities. A larger unit has 25 families; 100 families; 1000 families—

then regions and larger areas up to a national headquarters. Mutual benefit programmes are prepared to help members, patronising shops and services of other members.

It is not surprising that it is among the shopkeepers, the small businessmen and those in dangerous occupations (like mining) that the programme has its strongest appeal, similar to the early Methodist organisation. Moreover, in contrast to other religious organisations, the Soka Gakkai has had striking success with young people—having in May 1957 a Youth Corps of 120,000 young men and 70,000 young women. Despite the claims of its fascist tendencies, there is no evidence of a violent approach to change although the strong apocalyptic element in its teaching causes the leaders to paint lurid pictures of tragedies and disasters, attendant on non-acceptance of their teaching. The leaders are inclined to regard members as their 'children', who need care, rewards and happiness.

This new movement also expresses other insights, which have become apparent since the close of the Second World War. These insights have called for a greater flexibility in social organisation, so that there may be a useful blend of flexibility and discipline—especially in the light of Japanese culture. The flexibility is seen in the proliferation of groups among students, young wives, drama groups and others. But at the same time, there is a clear expression of the strong group-consciousness, providing and creating a community, under an authoritarian leadership. The strength of the primary groups in the households is used to build up a network of inter-relationships, reaching to the national headquarters itself. The values expressed through the beliefs of the movement are also simple enough to meet basic needs. The teaching is founded on the teaching of the early religious philosophers and therefore provides a sense of continuity with the past, particularly a Japanese past. It provides a simple cosmic explanation yet one which is not entirely new. Furthermore, the teaching is practical (this worldly) and emphasises the equality among the members, which is particularly relevant in the 'century of the common man'. The movement is in fact opposed to any attempt to revive the older Shinto beliefs, which strengthened and buttressed the imperial family. This is understandable as the leaders of the Soka Gakkai, in the war years, spent some years in prison as being opposed to the recognised and established forms of worship.

This account of the development of the Soka Gakkai religious and moral association is given to show the way in which religious organisations have expanded, on the one hand, and, on the other, have in some cases supported candidates for various public offices. The Soka Gakkai have been outstanding in this respect in their organisation and success.

4. Integration

Although a large number of Chinese have left their homes to settle in the West, there have only been a small number of Japanese who have done this. Most of the 30,000 Chinese immigrants in the United Kingdom have come from Commonwealth countries, in particular Hong Kong and Malaysia. The Chinese are mainly in three categories —the old emigrants (the seamen) who had emigrated to Britain between the wars; those who are businessmen, students and nurses; and thirdly, those who are employed in the restaurant business. Because of their specialised interests, these immigrants do not compete with the natives of the

British Isles, and their number is too insignificant to serve as a 'minority problem' to the host society.

There is therefore even less likelihood that the Japanese will cause a 'minority problem' in Western society. A large number of Japanese have settled in San Francisco and other Western cities in the United States. The close connection between the United States and Japan since the close of the Second World War has increased the number of Japanese who are visiting the States. Some Japanese women have married American soldiers and so the connections are brought closer. In Australia, as well as New Zealand, there has long been a fear lest the land-hungry islanders of Japan should have designs upon their territories, but, as with the United States, immigration laws keep a close watch on the number of those permitted to enter these countries from the more highly populated lands of the Asian mainland and islands. While the entrance of these new racial groups is carefully watched and controlled, there appears to be no pressing 'minority problem', although their highly fertile families may well make their numbers in a generation or so far more significant. It is their rate of population growth that is of major concern to white races.

During the past half-century, the practice of family planning has been widely adopted in Western countries and there has been a drop in the birth rate although (due to medical advance) there has been a rise in the number of live births and of those who survive. In the East, however, the adoption of family planning has only made slow progress. There have been strenuous efforts to provide training in hygiene and in modes of family control in India. In China, the population growth continues despite the famines and the natural calamities, which have not yet been mastered. In Japan, family loyalty still is expressed in large families to carry on the family name and responsibilities. But there is also a great limitation of land, so that the bulging population has to look for fresh fields to find room for expansion.

Despite the collapse of the war, the economy of Japan recovered quickly from the effects of the war. As a hard-working and industrious people, the Japanese were imitating the West in building factories and becoming highly industrialised. The result of their pre-war industry became evident in the speed with which they attacked and advanced into the mainland of China and then later attacked American bases at Pearl Harbour and in the Philippines. The white nations in the Pacific are well aware of the industrial progress of the Japanese and this, together with their high rate of fertility, makes them an object of suspicion lest they undercut the wages and labour of white people.

The ability of the Japanese to adapt and adopt the industrial techniques of the Western nations has been outstanding among nations of the East. On the other hand, there has not been the same development in other spheres, so that there are only one thousand welfare workers among 90 million people. There is a great shortage of medical services, which is serious in the midst of rapidly expanding urbanisation.

Summary

The dependence of one culture, isolated by geographical factors, upon others is clearly seen in regard to Japan. The isolation is also evident in the divisiveness which occurs in areas, which are widely separated in scattered islands and resent the influence which outside authorities may endeavour to exercise over them. On the other hand, the same geographic isolation may well contribute to a sturdy independence of thought, which takes pride in the individual contribution which their area can offer to the culture of the nation as a whole.

All these factors play their part in Japanese religion. The native cults were nature-centred and lacked qualities such as those provided by the longer culture of China, which itself was assisted and fertilised by the contact with India, which again was stimulated by the Indo-Aryan invasions and the contacts with Hellenic cultures in regard to art forms and other features. Denied this overland contact, Japan had to draw more particularly on those overseas contacts which were most open to her, namely, Korea and China, from which came Confucianism and Buddhism.

These beliefs were, however, accepted in accord with the demands of the local situation. The rise of powerful sects reflected the independency of thought and the isolation of areas, during the twelfth century and onwards. At the present time, the social needs of the people are similarly being met but in terms of a wide variety of religious groups, whose aims and purposes reveal the medley of past tradition and modern urbanised conceptions in a strange mixture. This blend of the old and the new is a commentary on the social situation, emerging into an era without precedent or clear light.

VI

ISLAM

1. Introduction

Islam forms a kind of belt which stretches round the earth from the Western shore of Africa to the islands of the East. This belt covers some areas south of the Equator, but in the main lies north of that line. 'Islam' is the name for the religion of Muhammad and is the infinitive of the Arabic verb 'to submit'. The term 'Muslim' refers to the one who follows that religion (and is the present participle of the same verb). Islam is not only a religion but is also used as a term to describe a particular blend of culture, which has taken up into itself a wide variety of other cultures. Many races and nations owe allegiance to Islam and turn towards Mecca as the sacred centre of their faith. It extends from the Atlantic to the Philippines and claims some three hundred million adherents. It includes the states of North Africa, of the Middle East, Pakistan, Persia, Turkey, parts of China and some of the Malay States.

As in the case of Hinduism, Islam has become closely linked with nationalism. This has meant that an Egyptian may not be a very ardent devotee of the doctrines of Muhammad the Prophet, but he would consider himself as part of Islam, which is the culture of his nation. The case of Turkey is even more interesting. In Turkey, many of the older practices, such as the veiling of women, have been legally abolished, yet the country would regard itself as part of Islam, though perhaps not as the leader of the Pan-Islamic nations in the way that the Sultan of Turkey regarded himself in earlier days. That role has been taken over mainly by Egypt, which has tried to express its loyalty to Islam while preserving its national identity, under President Nasser. Nevertheless, local practices, cultures and customs are widely prevalent in Islamic countries, however much there is a central loyalty to the teaching of the Prophet and to the sacred book, the *Qur'an*, in Arabic. The life of the Prophet and his own domestic practice have been widely followed. From his teaching came the sacred book of the faith and the basis of Islam, which includes the traditions and practices, such as are found to be honoured in widely separated cultures. Social customs have also grown up in accord with the schools of law, which are prominent in Islam.

2. The Prophet

The Prophet Muhammad was born about A.D. 570, and little is known about his early life. He came from the Quraysh tribe, which had special responsibility for the sanctuary (*Ka'ba*) at Mecca, in Arabia. The supreme tribal deity of this tribe was, probably, *Allah*, a male deity of whom Altat was the female counterpart. In the worship of his time, there were sacred stones (the *Ka'ba* shrine contained a black meteorite), sacred times and sacred seasons, especially in the spring when a 'pilgrimage festival' (*haj*) took place. Muhammad became a camel-master visiting various cities where he met Jews and Christians. He married a wealthy widow, Khadijah, who bore him several children, of whom only one daughter grew to maturity and had children of her own. (The heirs of this daughter, named Fatima, became the leaders of a large sect in Islam, called the Shi'a (the followers or sect of Ali, who married Fatima). This sect is strong in Persia.)

About the year A.D. 610, Muhammad became very restless and began to retire to the desert places outside Mecca. He also began to have visions and seizures and heard voices, which seemed to say to him: 'You are the chosen one; proclaim the name of the Lord.' Thus his call came to him as he meditated on Mount Hira. There followed a period of crisis, which extended over many months, but he was upheld by the encouragement of his wife, who believed in him and his mission. Then Muhammad began to proclaim his new beliefs—in the unity and sovereignty of Allah; the fiery Day of Judgment; the terrible fate of those who worshipped other gods and many gods but the bliss of those who were faithful in Paradise. He did not hesitate to attack the worship in the local shrine with its stone gods and there arose such fierce opposition that, in A.D. 622, Muhammad and his followers fled to the near-by town of Al Medina, where he established himself and built up his authority. This withdrawal (or *Hijra*) to Medina proved to be the turning-point in the Prophet's career and was chosen as the beginning of the Muslim era. (Thus the Muslim year, known as A.H., is obtained in A.D. by adding 622 and subtracting 3 for each Hijri century—to represent the difference between the lunar and solar year.)

Eventually, Muhammad was able to come to terms with the leaders in Mecca and returned there in triumph, in A.H. 8 (A.D. 630), where he ruled for two years until his death. He showed great clemency towards his former opponents in Mecca and even was generous towards them, in dividing later spoils with them. Thus, Islam became the religion of the State and wider political ambitions opened out before the Prophet. He showed kindness towards some of his former companions, by taking their widows under his care and made three important changes in the social life of his time—he abolished infanticide, he showed mercy to animals and he restrained, if not abolished, among his followers the use of wine.

The message of Muhammad brought unity and release to the polytheistic and divided tribal groups in Arabia. He made first and central his belief in the unity of Allah (God), who is seen as an absolute transcendent power, whose will is subject to none and is therefore arbitrary. There is no fixed moral standard, though it is believed that He is just. The whole duty of man is Islam (submission). As a result, man is deemed to be at his highest as a 'slave' (*abd*), totally submissive to the divine will. Such a conception of man has, in fact, produced a dignified and restrained type of character, which is resigned to circumstances as the expression of the will of Allah, who alone makes laws and gives all forms of blessing to mankind.

The teaching which followed from this message has proved very attractive for a number of reasons. There is the concept of the one true God, which appeals to many minds, especially in polytheistic lands, where many people are held in fear by the demands of many gods, some of which are capricious in their claims. From the servitude to many objects of worship, it is a relief to discover that one sovereign God of mercy rules in the affairs of men. This brings satisfaction to mental and devotional life. Furthermore, to accept the teaching of the Prophet opens the way into an

Islamic brotherhood, which, if not world-wide, embraces many lands. It can bring an end of conflict between warring tribes, as it is a serious sin to kill a brother Muslim without just cause. Also, in many African states, to embrace Islam means a rise in social prestige and status, which is made easier and more acceptable because the moral demands of Islam are not unduly exacting.

Many African tribes permit polygamy and Islam recognises this state of affairs in that four wives are legally permitted to a Muslim. It is recognised that a man should be economically able to support four wives, in that their sacred book (the *Qur'an*) enjoins that the husband should 'treat them equitably' (Sura IV. 3). This text has been the subject of some controversy as it has, in modern times, been interpreted to mean 'monogamy', on the ground that a man can only treat one 'equitably'. Moreover, some African states (as in the case of Ghana) have been endeavouring to establish monogamy or, at least, tighter marriage controls, to strengthen the family as a social unit. In any case, the transition from the extended family of the tribal society into Islam is easier than into Christianity, which has upheld firmly the principle of monogamous marriage, one man with one woman for life.

3. The Bases of Islam

The beliefs and practices of Islam are upheld by loyalty to the sacred book (the *Qur'an*), the traditions (*hadith*), the custom (the *sunna*) and the schools of law. The *Qur'an* is the record of the revelations which came to the Prophet and is the basis of the faith. The *Suras*, or chapters, grow longer and are more artificial towards the end of the life of Muhammad. The contents largely fall into two groups—those prophecies which were delivered in Mecca, and those in Medina. In regard to the first, there are few allusions to current events and it is difficult to date the various pieces, apart from matters of style. There is moral and religious earnestness and vigour in the earliest portions, which appears to be absent in the later period. The material from the Medina period has references to current events and, as the history is better known, it is easier to date the various sections.

As the revelations in the *Qur'an* extend over twenty years, it is not surprising that there is a variety of ideas and rules which were set down for the benefit of believers. For the first five centuries, it remained in the Arabic tongue before it was translated into other languages. Its importance lay, too, in the political expansion of Islam, as Muhammad was both prophet and ruler. The conquests of the Islamic soldiers made this book the guide in Church and State, which Islam has always regarded as one.

The *Qur'an* does not stand alone. Whenever a great man dies, there is an interest in his growth and development. In the case of Muhammad, he was regarded as the model for the true believer (who wished to know as much detail as possible about the prophet for his own guidance for life) and it was also necessary to supplement the *Qur'an* with further laws to aid the new state in Arabia. Therefore, there arose a collection of traditions about the prophet, and these traditions were known as the *hadith*. Many of these came from his Companions (of his generation) and from his Followers (the next generation) but were retained for some period by word of mouth and oral tradition.

It became necessary to have some reliable evidence in regard to these traditions and so each tradition came to be accompanied by a line of guarantors, the authorities on which they were based. As a result, there are various classes of traditions, whether they are sound, respectable or weak. If there are weak links then the trustworthiness of the tradition decreases. By such information, it was hoped to secure further help and guidance from the life and teaching of the prophet. In the main, the *Qur'an* is regarded as superior to tradition, though the community would normally seek to interpret the *Qur'an* to ensure that its interpretation is acceptable. As an infallible book, all truth must be found somewhere within it.

Together with the *hadith*, there is the *sunna*, the custom which finds expression in the whole way of life which the pious Muslim will try to follow. The *sunna* naturally includes such pious practices as it is believed that the prophet himself used. As a way of life, it has had a powerful impact on the culture of many lands. The care of Muhammad for children, his respect for the elderly and for orphans, and various other details of his life and practice, these have been narrated in the lives of the prophet in several languages, whose peoples have sought to model their lives on his practice.

At the same time, the *sunna* includes the customary practice of the particular local culture, which receives endorsement from the authority of religion. Thus, in some areas, it is rigidly enforced that the women should be veiled (on the authority of Sura XXXIII. 53), especially in Arabia itself, while elsewhere, as in the Malay States and in some tribal areas in Mongolia, there has been much greater freedom in this matter. In Turkey, for instance, the veil has been abolished altogether. Much of the *sunna* became hardened into customary law, which affected such issues as those of inheritance, although in this matter specific details were laid down in the *Qur'an*.

These bases of the life of the Muslim community were defined by the schools of law. These bases consisted of the *Qur'an*, the traditions, the use of analogy and the agreement of the community (*ijma*). If a practice or a belief was adopted by the community, it is agreed to be good Islam. However, there have always been many grounds for disagreement, so four schools of law have come to be acknowledged as the orthodox interpreters of Islamic law. Various sects in Islam emphasise the teaching of one or other of these schools, whose rulings are regarded as the final authorities in all matters of dispute.

The *Qur'an* itself contains some laws, such as those which give guidance on inheritance, on marriage, on interest, on debt and the duties of witnesses. A larger body of law developed slowly as decisions became necessary on knotty problems. In Arabia, as elsewhere, the local customary law was followed so long as it did not conflict with that of Islam and when conflict arose between customary law and the *Qur'an*, then reference had to be made to other authorities to settle the matter. The founders of the four schools of law were Abu Hanifa (a Persian, who developed his system in Iraqi and died in 676); Malik ibn Anas (who lived and worked in Medina, where he died in 795); Shafi'i (whose system is less free than that of Abu Hanifa, and more flexible than the stiff traditional views of Malik ibn Anas. He died in 820); and finally, there is the strongly traditionalist system of Ibn Hanbal (who died in 855 and resisted all innovations which failed to come close to the *Qur'an* and the *sunna*). All these four schools are equally orthodox and every *sunni* Muslim belongs to one of them. The *sunni*

Muslim is the orthodox party in Islam, in contrast to various sects which have arisen in different lands, of which the largest and most important is the *Shi'a* sect, which is very powerful in Iraq, Persia and North India. These sects believe in the unity of God and in the prophets but they also believe in the important place of *imams*, the accredited successors of the prophets. These sects, such as the *Zaidi* (in the Yemen), the *Isma'ilis* (under the leadership of the Aga Khan), the *Qarmati* (in Iraq), the *Nusairi* (in Northern Syria) and others, normally have their collection of traditions, their exegesis of the *Qur'an*, their system of law and their own way of life (i.e. their *sunna*).

4. Religious Practice

There are five pillars of Islam. These are faith, prayer, almsgiving, fasting and pilgrimage. There was an endeavour to add a sixth, the holy war, but this did not succeed. The Faith is summarised in the statement: 'There is no god but Allah, and Muhammad is the apostle of Allah.' This belief is in the one God, who is the creator and the absolute ruler of all things—free from passion, pain and from change. Muhammad is the last prophet and has given to men the final revelation which God desires to give to men. (As the prophet has a prominent place in Islam, this belief in the final word through Muhammad has resulted in many conflicts, as various prophets have appeared in different parts of Islam. In particular, among the Shi'a sect, there is a widespread belief that the imams are successors of the prophet as interpreters of the *Qur'an*.)

The obligation of prayer covers the wider concept of

worship, for which the worshipper has to be ritually clean. Religious custom has defined in minutest detail the ablutions necessary to be 'clean'. There are five daily prayers: before dawn, afternoon, in the middle of the afternoon (at the time when a stick casts a shadow of its own length), after sunset and after dark. These five periods are not mentioned in the *Qur'an* but certainly belong to the earliest period of Islam. Each prayer consists of two or more sections (having Qur'anic phrases and passages) with an epilogue. The prayers are recited in various attitudes—standing, squatting, bowing and sometimes with the forehead touching the ground. The place of prayer must be clean and therefore it is customary to remove one's shoes before entering a mosque. Prayers are said facing Mecca, so mosques are usually built with their main axis pointing to Mecca. It is obligatory to keep the midday prayer on Friday in the mosque.

The noon prayer on Friday consists of two sections which are normally preceded by the sermon, which is, however, also preceded by a prayer. It is meritorious to keep all one's prayers in the mosque but at the proper time, lest the prayer be not valid. In early days, women were permitted to attend the mosque and took their place behind the men, but this does not take place now. While prayer is meritorious in the mosque, yet it is also an individual act. This is recognised in that, when prayer takes place in the open, a man will place his shoes or his rifle in front of him, to serve as a 'fence' to his place of prayer. Many sayings exhort the faithful to be loyal to this obligation of prayer—'What is the best act? Prayer at the right time.' 'Prayer is the key to paradise.' Even in the conditions of war, an army may divide its forces, so that one half stands to arms while the other half is engaged in prayer.

The third pillar is almsgiving, which covers all forms of religious taxes. Muhammad insisted on the necessity of hospitality and the exercise of charity towards the needy. He later went on to fix a minimum amount by law, which came to be defined in detail according to a man's possessions. As the community was essentially a pastoral one, the allocation of tax was in terms of a man's flocks and herds. Therefore, if a man owned from five to nine camels, he was called upon to pay one sheep. If he owned twenty-five to thirty-five camels, then he was expected to pay one female yearling camel. In the case of money, the man who owned twenty gold dinars was expected to pay five per cent of his capital. In early times, the tax camels were collected by the state and used for its wars but there was later controversy whether almsgiving should be collected by the state or whether it was a man's own responsibility to distribute his own alms. It is customary, in any case, for pious Muslims to distribute their own alms.

The fourth pillar is fasting. The whole of the ninth month, known as *Ramadan*, is ordained as a fast. During each day of this period, from the time when it is possible to distinguish a white thread from a black one until sunset, the believer must abstain from eating, drinking, from having sexual intercourse and, in recent times, from smoking. Certain persons are excused, namely, children, pregnant women, the sick, the aged and travellers—although, in the case of the last, they are expected to fast the equivalent number of days at another time. This period of fast is now fixed by the calendar. During this period, the Muslim towns are fascinatingly ordered, since traders and shops flourish after sunset until the morning, when the fast begins again.

Various interpretations are given to the meaning of the

fast, namely, that it enables the rich to sympathise with the poor; that it is a useful discipline; that it also means the avoidance of mean desires and worldliness; and that this fast blots out sins which have been committed during the previous year. Such a fast in a hot Arabian or Indian climate requires great self-control but it is also common to find that there are voluntary fasts at other periods of the year. On the other hand, it is regarded as a sin to fast during a festival and it is also meritorious to distribute alms at the close of the month of Ramadan.

The fifth pillar is the obligation to make a pilgrimage. In pre-Islamic days, there were two religious rites connected with Mecca. One of these consisted in walking seven times round the Ka'ba and seven times round two raised mounds known as *Safa* and *Marwa*—this rite was known as 'the little pilgrimage'. The second rite was the pilgrimage to 'Arafat, a little hill about sixteen miles to the east of Mecca. Islam has combined these two rites in a pilgrimage, which is regarded as the duty of every Muslim, on condition that he is of sound mind, of fit age and can afford the journey.

Every pious Muslim expects to make the pilgrimage to Mecca at least once in his lifetime. There is prescribed a certain pilgrim dress, which, in the case of a man, consists of two lengths of unsewn cloth which leave bare the arms and the right shoulder. For a woman pilgrim, the correct dress is a large cotton cloth garment, which covers the person completely but without the veil, which is replaced by a mask. The head is bare but, with the intense heat, umbrellas are allowed. It is considered desirable that the pilgrim should wear this dress from the beginning of the pilgrimage, but this is interpreted by most to mean the point near

Mecca, where pillars on the main routes indicate where the pilgrimage garments should be worn. The various details of the pilgrimage have become customary month by month, so that the pattern of the pilgrimage is plain and straightforward for all the pilgrims.

When the pilgrims arrive, they carry out the rites of the little pilgrimage. On the seventh day of the month, a sermon is delivered in the mosque and then the pilgrims proceed to Muna, where the morning prayer is said on the following day. On the ninth day, they have to be in 'Arafat, where they wait from noon till sunset. This waiting time is regarded as an essential discipline in the act of the pilgrim. There follows a hurried journey to Muzdalifa—on the return to Mecca—where the combined sunset and night prayers are said. There also the pilgrims share in the morning prayer on the tenth, when the crowd move on to Muna where they all throw seven stones at each of three pillars—an action known as 'the stoning of the pass'. Here it is customary for sacrifices to be killed and for the men to shave their heads. The pilgrims then resume their normal dress but proceed to Mecca, where they march around the Ka'ba, which is also part of the final ceremony, which includes the march between the two hills (*Safa* and *Marwa*), when the pilgrims wear again their pilgrim dress.

The area of Mecca itself is regarded as sacred, so that various activities are forbidden there, including hunting, the cutting of wood as well as (for pilgrims) the contracting of marriages and acting as witnesses and (for men) the wearing of ornamental rings, the use of perfume and to cut one's hair. It is the great ambition as well as the obligation of every Muslim to make the pilgrimage to Mecca. Every year many thousands cross the Red Sea from Africa or travel from Pakistan and beyond to visit the holy places in Arabia.

There has been an endeavour to add 'the holy war' as an additional obligation. The *Qur'an* gives sanction to war against unbelievers. Many took part in the conquests, though some ascetics would refuse to take their share in the booty. The law schools have laid down the conditions upon which the holy war may become an obligation. These conditions include that the unbelievers must begin the hostilities, it should be sanctioned by a duly constituted *imam*, there should be a reasonable expectation of success and a determination to win. The warrior who died in such a holy war was considered to be a martyr whose soul would be straightway transported to paradise. At the same time, it is recognised that the major battle for the believer is the internal one against sin.

Various other practices have become customary (*sunna*). It is common to fast on Tuesdays and Thursdays. During the month of Ramadan, special prayers are said during the earlier part of the night. These prayers differ according to the sects, so that, for example, among the *Shi'a*, the prayers are divided into one thousand sections, which are spread over the whole month. In the course of these prayers, some pious Muslims repeat the whole of the *Qur'an* once or more frequently. Eclipses and periods of drought call forth special prayers.

It is also possible to carry out these acts on behalf of another. For example, it is permitted to give alms and to go on pilgrimage on behalf of a dead person. Such acts serve to give merit to the one who carries them out—as a pious act. Similarly, a man may make the pilgrimage to Mecca on behalf of his aged father or grandfather. The man who actually makes the journey, in this instance, cannot call himself a pilgrim but does acquire for himself the merit of assisting a fellow Muslim in fulfilling the faith. As in many religions, it is the practice of men and women in Islam 'to go into retreat'. During such a period, there is a time of fasting and, for a man, the retreat takes place in a mosque. It is not permitted during this period of retreat, which is often in fulfilment of a vow, for the retreatant to visit the sick, pray over a corpse or conduct his normal business.

5. Social Custom

It is important in the sects of Islam to keep to various food laws. In the numerous *Shi'a* sect, food prepared by Christians or Jews is unlawful as also are eels and certain vegetables. This must inevitably create difficulties in buying meat (for example) in Christian lands. The *Zaidi* section of the *Shi'a*, who live in the Yemen, regard the flesh of all animals slaughtered by non-Muslims as unclean. Among the *Nusairi*, who live in Northern Syria, they abstain from eating camels, hares, eels and other delicacies, such as crabs, gazelles, porcupines and tomatoes. In general, uncleanness is attached to certain foods, which means that they must not be used for food. Pork, carrion and blood are thus regarded as unclean in themselves, as also are most dogs. The flesh of all animals which are not slaughtered according to the law is unclean. It is therefore necessary for a strict Muslim to decline invitations to eat in another's house, as it is difficult to ensure purity of food.

Carrion is defined as any animal which has been killed by another or by accident or has died naturally, which therefore means that it has not been slaughtered according to the law. Blood is forbidden among many peoples as food, as also in the Old Testament. It is also forbidden to drink intoxicant drinks, especially wine which is forbidden in the *Qur'an*. Nevertheless, many of the caliphs used to drink freely. There are various local drinks, which are made from dates and honey and are fermented and widely used, though some of the law schools forbid them.

Food is normally taken with the fingers, so the hands are washed before and after meals. The left hand must not be used for eating, as it is used for unclean purposes. If a guest inadvertently places his left hand into a bowl of food, the host would be too polite to rebuke him but would probably quietly order that the bowl should be removed and thrown away. In the desert where the lack of water made washing difficult, it was customary to wipe the hands on the tent wall before the door. It is therefore a mark of honour to see a thick coat of grease there, as it indicates that the owner of the tent is a man of hospitality and generosity.

Hospitality has a large place as one of the chief virtues, and travellers were sheltered and protected by the chief or the headman of a village as his duty. A change has taken place in more recent times with the coming of more visitors and hotels, when modes of travel have made travellers from greater distances more frequent. These social expressions of faith are kept within the measure of the orthodoxy of the family, when the members live in the Western world. It is natural that members of the Islamic faith should endeavour to keep close together as a community and that they should seek to keep true to their faith, whatever may be the change in environment.

6. Problems of Immigration

During the past few years, there has been an increasing number of Muslims who have entered Britain from the Turkish areas in Cyprus (after the independence movement there) and from Pakistan. Some have also come from West Africa and Kenya. These immigrants have differed in social standing and education from the very much smaller number which came earlier as students and who expected to return to their native lands as professional men, for example, to Nigeria and to Pakistan, as lawyers, doctors and teachers. Many of the immigrants have come to make their homes in this country and their children are forming a large part of the school population in Birmingham, Wolverhampton and in other areas. The lack of professional and technical training makes it necessary for many of the fathers of these families to take non-skilled jobs, for which wages are low, while the costs of living and of housing accommodation increase.

Many hospitals and transport services are only able to carry on because these workers have come. It is, however, important to recognise that their continued place in the British community will mean that their life as minorities will require adjustments from their previous culture to the kind of life which they find in Britain. Their children will wish to be accepted by their playmates and will find a conflict in many cases between the rules of the old culture (and religion) and the customs and habits of those around them. The result will no doubt be that some families will hold on more firmly to the old, while others will be more easy-going and tolerant. Many families will seek a compromise which will help them to keep true to the best in the old way while sharing the advantages of the new way of life.

Summary

The respect for the teaching of the Prophet will continue to have an important place in the thought and the affections of the Muslim world. The study of Arabic will still open the way to a deeper understanding of the *Qur'an* but it will be increasingly difficult for Arabic to hold its place when English, Russian and other languages are used in the communication of scientific knowledge. Urbanisation will mean increased communication, which will include radio and television, in which the more wealthy nations will tend to occupy the channels. The pressure from Western cultures is therefore likely to grow and make loyalty to the older religious cultures more difficult.

This impact in communication will affect not only the subject of language. The use of Arabic as a *lingua franca* in the Middle East may decline as nationalist movements develop and this will influence the unity of Islam. The growth of secularism is expected to affect religious belief in the *Qur'an* and therefore the *sunna* and *hadith*, which are connected with it. Loyalty to food customs will be upheld by the orthodox but the less loyal believers, when they move into other cultures and are affected by scientific thought, are liable to be more 'liberal' and less devoted to earlier custom. Their children are even less likely to retain a desire to keep 'food laws' and other Islamic practices, which will differentiate them from the culture in which these families have come to make their permanent home. In the moral field, it is to be expected that women will continue to have a greater freedom; marriage by partners' choice will be more widely accepted and education for all will become the rule. It is also probable that the Muslim will accept monogamy as the common practice in marriage to a greater extent than previously.

VII

JUDAISM AND CHRISTIANITY

1. Introduction

It is fitting that these two faiths should be considered together even though they have often been in bitter conflict and persecuted each other. They both stem from a foundation of basic beliefs and their later developments have sprung from the differing outworkings of these basic beliefs. The nature of the One God, who is active in history and makes known his purposes in the affairs of man and nature, serves as the root from which very varied fruits have grown. The early development is set forth in the record of the Old Testament, which describes the historical growth of the Hebrew nation over a period of some two thousand years and more. Its early records were the tales narrated round the camp-fires, from father to son, for many generations before they were set down in written form.

When the tribes, which believed themselves to be descended from certain common ancestors, named as Abraham, Isaac and Jacob, were welded together into a nation and became a kingdom, there arose the desire to write down in more permanent form the history of the nation. In the pre-literary period, the religion of the Hebrew people was very similar to other Semite peoples, which were related to them. There was the belief in many sacred beings (or polydaemonism). There are references to the beliefs of the tribes in the days before the Conquest of Canaan (Joshua *24*.14) as well as in the land of Canaan itself (as may be seen from the following verse). It was a religion of agriculturists, of *Baals*, in which fertility cults played a large part. The festivals celebrated the cycle in nature, with rituals which had the theme of a dying deity who revived in the spring-time.

When the Hebrew tribes, which entered the land of Palestine in a succession of invasions as well as some who appear to have been resident there from an early period, were united and strong enough to seek common leadership, there developed the institution of kingship, especially under David who, about the year 1000 B.C., captured the Jebusite fortress of Jerusalem and made it the capital of the country. Under the reign of his son, Solomon, there were grave tensions, which resulted in the division of the kingdom (about 930 B.C.) into the two kingdoms—the Northern kingdom of Israel and the Southern kingdom of Judah. The latter continued to remain faithful to the house of David. These two kingdoms were continually under pressure from the great powers, which were to the north and south, namely, Assyria and Egypt. Moreover, the Northern kingdom was frequently at war with its neighbours, the kingdoms of Syria and Moab, although the smaller kingdoms combined at times against the larger agression of Assyria.

The Northern kingdom of Israel was eventually destroyed, together with her neighbours, by the Assyrian conqueror Tiglath-pileser III, whose armies dispersed the inhabitants in Media to the east, during the years 726–720 B.C. The Southern Kingdom of Judah managed to survive for another one hundred and forty years, until the rise of the Babylonian

Empire under Nebuchadnezzar, who eventually destroyed Jerusalem in 586 B.C. The inhabitants of the Southern kingdom were taken to Babylon in two stages. In 596 B.C., the leading citizens (including the king and his court) and the craftsmen were taken and then, ten years later, another large contingent was taken to Babylon. The first group retained a strong sense of solidarity and remained as the hope of a 'Remnant', whose restoration would fulfil the former dreams of national glory.

While there are similarities between the early religion of the Hebrews and their neighbours, yet it is in the dissimilarities in their beliefs and practices that the future development lies. It is difficult to establish how early in their history they believed in a 'special relationship' or a covenant between their deity and themselves. Certainly, by the time of the great leader Moses (about 1280 B.C.), there appears to have been established a relationship, with specific terms on the part of Israel, with their God Yahweh, whose leadership was seen in a succession of judges, prophets and priests, by whom the people were led in their movement into the land of Palestine.

The 'Covenant-relationship' also operated through the kings, especially in the Southern Kingdom, where the house of David tried to keep loyal to the covenant made by David with his God and his people at the beginning of his reign (2 Samuel 5. 3). While there were demands set down to ensure the loyalty of the people of Israel to their God, the nature of Yahweh remained hidden. Under the leadership of a great succession of prophets, Yahweh's demands came to reveal a moral quality, which differed greatly from that of the deities in neighbouring lands.

Just as in the stories of Abraham (especially in Genesis

22) there is evidence that human sacrifice came to be discountenanced in Israel, so the moral practices of the fertility gods also came under the condemnation of her prophets. There came to be a clear break with the ethnic gods of blood and soil as Yahweh came to be seen as Lord of Righteousness, concerned with justice and morality—both within the nation of the Hebrews and in her relationships with other nations. This break with ethnic cults enabled the Hebrews to continue to believe in the power and wisdom of their deity, despite their own defeats and disasters, which did not necessarily mean His defeat.

In the teaching of these Hebrew prophets, the character and activity of Yahweh were expressed very clearly. While Yahweh was supremely the God of Israel, His rule ran throughout creation. Therefore He is Lord of Nature and and could be trusted as seen in Nature's laws. In fact, He is Law in that He is utterly trustworthy. As He is the beginning, so also He is the fulfilment of all creation. In relation to men, He is seen, not only in Nature, but also in Moral Law and as Lord of History. Moral law is not confined to Israel but to all nations, so the prophet Amos condemned Moab for her treatment of the king of Edom, just as he also condemned Israel for her injustices. Thus, these prophets brought into close relationship devotion to Yahweh and just treatment between man and man. Yahweh would not be content unless the actions of the market-place and of the law-courts were just and in accord with His character of justice (Amos *8*. 5, 6).

Another important contribution of the Hebrew prophets was their attitude to the temple sacrifice and the ritual demands of contemporary religion. It seems probable that they did not condemn outright all ritual practices of their day (which included the offering of many kinds of animals, in burnt offerings and peace offerings, as well as grain in the cereal offerings), yet the prophets strongly condemned such sacrifices unless they were accompanied by righteousness of life. They recognised that such sacrifices might prove an opiate to the consciences of the people (especially the wealthy), while untold suffering was the lot of the poor, the landless and those in need. In this regard, the Hebrew prophets were widely separated in approach from other religions of their time. They saw sin, not as did so many other Israelites as the commitment of a breach in ritual, but as the violation of a moral law. Such a conception eventually would result in superseding the older sacrificial order; but this came much later.

During the period of the Exile (596–538 B.C.), the Hebrews came to see even more clearly some of the implications of their convictions. The One God, to whom alone they must give allegiance, came to be seen not only as the All-Righteous and All-Merciful, but also as the Ruler and God of the Nations. This was seen clearly by the great Prophet of the Exile, who proclaimed that the Median conqueror Cyrus had been raised up by Yahweh to subdue the nations and to overcome the opponents of Israel (Isaiah 45. 1–5). The people of Israel hoped that their opponents would be defeated and that their ancient glories (of Davidic days) would be restored to them. In the cities of their exile, they held firmly to their belief that they would be the 'chosen people', the bearer of the truth of their God to all the nations.

This belief came to take two forms of expression. In the first place, when the exiles were permitted to return home from Babylon to Jerusalem, the loyal returned families did settle down with those who had come to live there during their absence. But, under Nehemiah and Ezra, a powerful movement to separate the returned exiles from 'the people of the land' took place. Inter-marriage was forbidden and the community in Jerusalem sought to preserve its spiritual and religious heritage by strict laws. This separatism became increasingly exclusive and heightened the tensions in Palestine, creating gulfs which deepened with the years. The irreconcilability of the Jews and Samaritans was one result of this separatist policy. Every attempt was made to preserve inviolate the heritage of 'the Returned', who were identified as 'the Redeemed', through whom (it was believed) the fulfilment of the Lord's promises would come. Despite the pressures of the Persian satraps and overlords, as well as the demands of Greek and Seleucid rulers, the community in Jerusalem retained their exclusive devotion to their faith in Yahweh.

On the other hand, there were those among the returned exiles who believed that the mission of Israel included non-Israelites. This view is seen in the books of *Ruth* and *Jonah* which are pleas for a wider hope to include other nations. *Ruth* describes the faithfulness of a Moabite woman, whose devotion to Yahweh and to her Israelite family was rewarded in an outstanding way, in that she was an ancestress of the great King David. *Jonah* was a 'tract for the times', using the figure of an earlier prophet to plead for the sinful and cruel capital (Nineveh) of the mighty Assyrian Empire to be destroyed, only to be admonished by Yahweh for his failure in mercy towards the pagan city. This view that the privileges of Israel should be shared with other nations fell on deaf ears, however, as the Jerusalem community put up religious and physical walls to protect themselves from the heathen nations beyond. The buttress for this separation lay in the Law, whose provisions gave direction to the lives of individuals by means of the amplifications and explanations provided by successive generations of scribes and Pharisees.

When the rulers of Syria sought to force the Jews (as this community came to be called) to accept Greek ways of worship, the Maccabean War (167 B.C.) strengthened the Jewish determination to secure and maintain their independence, which was recognised in 143/2 B.C. This period of native rule lasted for the period, 134–65 B.C., under the Hasmonean rulers, but the Roman arms were too strong to be resisted and finally, in A.D. 70, Jerusalem was destroyed, after several attempts to secure her freedom from Rome. But during all this period, from the time of the Exile onwards, it is important to remember that the Jewish community which had remained in the cities of the old Babylonian Empire and in cities in Asia Minor as well as in Egypt, continued to live according to the Law and was loyal to the older ways of worship and practice.

After the fall of Jerusalem, the Jews remained in their 'Dispersion' throughout the cities of the Roman Empire and further East in the lands which lay in Parthia. While the early Christian Church was regarded at first as 'the sect of the Nazarenes', a Jewish sect, it was thereby admitted as a legitimate religion, having the privileges which the Caesars gave to the Jews at a costly price. However, when Jerusalem fell and the Jewish rabbis settled at Jamnia, in contrast to the Christian leaders who went to Pella, it became clear that the Jewish community and the Christian community were quite distinct, and henceforward both went their own separate ways.

Although the Jews of the Dispersion carried on their business among their neighbours after A.D. 70 there was still some resistance in some cities, such as Alexandria, and in Cyprus, and at length, under Bar-Kokhba, in Palestine, which was finally subdued by Roman arms in A.D. 135, after which date the Romans forbade any Jew, on pain of death, to dwell in or to enter Jerusalem. From this time, when the Jewish communities were 'aliens in a heathen world', they carried on their life under the leadership of the Pharisees, men like Johanan ben Zakkai, whose sober devotion to the Law of Moses brought fresh hope to the Jews. Insufficient attention has been given to the contribution, which these Jewish communities have given to later cultures, whether in Christendom of the Middle Ages or in Muslim lands or in later industrial and technological cultures. These communities were often hounded from city to city and land to land, yet they maintained their own self-government and family loyalty wherever they came. They upheld their devotion to an ethical monotheism with a dignified morality which was the envy of Gentile neighbours. Much has still to be written on their great intellectual commercial and religious contribution to mankind.

While the Christian religion has sprung from Jewish foundations, yet it is very difficult to do adequate justice to the development of Christianity within a brief compass. It would therefore be helpful to divide the subject into (a) the early development, (b) formative phases in its history and (c) aspects of modern developments.

(a) *The Early Development*

As with most religious movements, there is normally some outstanding personality, who serves to focus the teaching and aspirations of his followers. Although Judaism had long been led by a succession of prophets, such leaders appeared less frequently after the Exile and were more frequently found in social and political fields as well as religious ones. However the personality of the central character of the Christian religion (Jesus of Nazareth) is interpreted, there can be little doubt that he had a creative mind which brought together many of the deepest insights of the Jewish faith. Moreover, while there appears to be little doubt that Jesus was a genuine historical person (unlike the legendary figure of Mithras, the Persian god of truth), there was a remarkable diffidence on the part of his immediate followers to use terms which would normally be applied to a learned teacher. He was seen as more than 'rabbi' and 'more than a prophet', namely, as one who had a quality of uniqueness which lifted his life and practice beyond the human level, so that men, even in his presence, felt that sense of awe which is associated with the divine. Perhaps a supreme example of this uniqueness lay in the union between teaching and practice, which characterised Jesus of Nazareth. His actual ministry was short, probably less than two years, yet throughout it he expressed the truths spoken by parable and paradox by the peerless quality of his example. It is not a matter for surprise that miraculous stories should circulate about him from an early period.

The facts of the life of Jesus of Nazareth are comparatively few. His birth took place probably about the sixth year before the beginning of the Christian era, and the year of his death, by crucifixion, was probably in A.D. 29 when he was aged thirty-four or thirty-five. From the record of his infancy, found in the New Testament, his birth took place in Bethlehem, a village near Jerusalem, to which his parents had gone on the occasion of a census. Eventually his parents returned to the northern province of Galilee, to the town of Nazareth, where he appears to have spent most of his life, presumably in the occupation of a carpenter, with which his family was associated. When he began to preach, he appears to have moved to the city of Capernaum, where he gathered around him fishermen and others as disciples. Although his family lived in humble circumstances, there is reason to believe that the family came from the royal lineage of the Davidic family, which is found in the two genealogies in the Gospels of Matthew and Luke.

Many aspects of his life (and the traditions associated with it) have been debated. Thus, for example, there have been grave questions raised by the story of his Virgin Birth. Such a story appears to have arisen at a late date, probably after the close of the century, yet its congruity with the rest of the life of Jesus has made it more easily acceptable. It underlined the true humanity of Jesus, of whom many claimed that he was not 'real' but only an 'appearance'. It also emphasised his uniqueness which had already been realised in his life and teaching. Other stories, such as the flight into Egypt, may well have found their place in the record through the influence of foreshadowings or proof-texts from the Old Testament, which carried much weight in the early Christian circles.

With regard to his actual public ministry, it appears that there was a period of twelve months, mainly in the North in Galilee, during which most of his teaching to the crowds took place, and then there came a period of some nine months, during which he gave more attention to the training of the twelve and the other disciples, which culminated in the final journey to Jerusalem, probably in the month of April. This journey followed the incident when Jesus and the Twelve Apostles went to Caesarea Philippi and Peter made his confession of faith in Jesus as the Messiah. This title Jesus accepted with reservations and an interpretation of his own. The view of the Messiah as a conquering military hero he decisively rejected, and in place of it he chose to identify the Messianic role with that of the Suffering Servant, through whose sufferings the nations were to be redeemed.

Previously, the nation of Israel regarded itself as the Suffering Servant but Jesus took this image to himself as part of his world-wide mission to proclaim the Kingdom of God, whose healing presence was revealed by the works of compassion and healing which he did. There is little doubt that this confession of Peter was a turning-point in his ministry and found expression also in the event of the transfiguration. The Sermon on the Mount, the parables and his other teaching received their endorsement and authority from the kind of person he was, particularly in the manner of his death, of which the details were retained in great detail by his disciples.

The attraction of Jesus from the days of his flesh until the present time has been seen by Christians as the impact of his victorious life, which in its stark close by crucifixion is seen as a supreme act of God. Discussion will remain on the meaning of the Resurrection of Jesus, yet this also is seen as part of the one great event. There needs also to be taken into account, however, not only the so-called 'Resurrection appearances' but other events, such as the Ascension, the conversion of St. Paul and the visions of those of later times (such as Pascal and the Sadhu Sundar Singh) as well as the experiences of very many ordinary Christian people over the centuries, for whom the evidence of a risen and living Jesus is authentic and veridical, apart from any particular interpretation about an empty tomb.

The death of the prophetic leader of this new movement within Judaism did not stop the spread of his ideas. The very extent of the Jewish dispersion, with synagogues and praying-places in so many cities around the Mediterranean, made the spread of such ideas so much the faster. The rise of an able Jew from Tarsus to a place of leadership, following his conversion, only served to give drive and direction to the move outward from Palestine into the Gentile world. From a new base in Antioch, the missionary leaders travelled into the cities of Asia Minor, Greece and Italy, where their ideas found a ready soil for expansion and growth.

It needs also to be remembered that there were a great number of other Oriental cults, many of them from Asia Minor, which were pouring into Rome during the same period, so that the Christian movement received a ready reception along with many other cults at a time when there was much insecurity and lack of personal identity. Any 'salvation cult' was welcomed in the midst of a society where a vast empire made the individual feel helpless in the face of impersonal forces and far-away authority. Moreover, the moral appeal of this faith, with its high standard in marriage and family life, was carried on from its Jewish heritage but without the food restrictions, circumcision and other features which Gentiles disliked.

Certain features about this faith differentiated it from others. Firstly, the continuity with Jewish monotheism gave deep roots in history to the new movement. It claimed to be the true heir of the older promises but it now made available to all nations a heritage which had previously been regarded as the preserve of the Jewish people alone.

Secondly, in the account of the world as the creation of One God, the highest expression of his will is to be found in the person of Jesus, who fully embodied 'The Way', as Christianity was designated in the early days. This Jesus was seen to be the fullest expression of the divine nature, in so far as humans could perceive him.

Thirdly, there was full and complete emphasis on the humanity of Jesus, whose hunger, thirst, weariness and suffering were never other than the tribulations of a truly human life, such as other human beings can share. In this regard, the Christian emphasis on his death 'under Pontius Pilate' played an important part, when many of the competing Mystery-religions were rooted in nature-myths which had no roots in the 'flesh and blood' of history.

Fourthly, this message—proclaimed as Good News— gave a new dignity to human life. In contrast to other religions, this religion proclaimed the dignity of human life, since everyday decisions were fraught with eternal conse- quences, which took as their criterion the judgment of the Jesus, whose compassion had been experienced in history. Moreover, in his company, women as well as men were welcomed—in contrast to other contemporary religions, which had little or no place for one of the other sex. Dignity in human relationships, towards marriage and to the humbler ranks in society, sprang from the new concep- tion of the terms 'in Christ', which embraced Jew, Samari- tan, pagan and slave alike. This new relationship formed the basis of the Fellowship (*koinonia*), in which those of all nations and classes were invited to participate.

The strong Hebrew background of this faith provided a

strength and an exclusiveness, which resulted in due time in fierce persecution. The Roman authorities opposed this faith which was unwilling to give sacrifices to the Emperor as though he were a deity. Such unwillingness prevented Christians from holding some public offices and, in some cases soldiers from serving in the Army. Some emperors endeavoured to stamp out the Christian communities in various parts of the Empire. However, it grew as an underground movement, nurtured by little books (including the letters of Paul of Tarsus and accounts of the life and teaching of Jesus) and also by a growing firmness of structure in organisation, which could give direction and encouragement. While in very early days, those of poorer ranks of society were attracted to the ranks of this new movement, there was an increasing number of those of better position who were desirous of embracing the doctrines of this faith, which brought a clean and wholesome view of God, man and society, without the tiresome restrictions which the older Jewish faith required from believer and proselyte alike.

The use of buildings was often difficult, because the Church was an outlawed organisation, yet secret meetings were held frequently (such as before the dawn) and messengers passed from church to church, whether in the course of army duty, of commercial enterprise, or as slaves who were carrying out commands for their masters. It is not altogether clear to what extent the congregations were continuously harassed but it is probable that such persecutions were spasmodic, depending on the arrival of a particularly officious individual or a new edict from Rome, which only happened from time to time. A quiet growth in strength and numbers appears to have been the general pattern.

Under the leadership of bishops and presbyters, the organisation was able to meet challenges which came from several directions. The challenge from outside came from political powers and from other alternative faiths (like Mithraism), which had sacraments and practices which closely resembled Christian ones. The challenge from within came from conflict over the two natures of Christ as human and divine and from the clash between Greek thought and the Hebraeo-Christian concepts, which came into the open in the great councils of the Church.

Eventually, in A.D. 314, by the Edict of Milan, the Emperor Constantine agreed to accept the Christian Faith and to make it the official faith of the Empire. The bishops were able to have greater freedom in the care of their dioceses and the Church could move out more easily to carry out its programme to bring all men into the Kingdom of God. This meant privilege and power and within seventy years it became the recognised legal form of religion within the Empire. Even in its unorthodox form, as Arianism, it exercised considerable influence as it moved out to the Goths and Vandals and beyond the confines of the Empire to form churches in Armenia and Georgia as well as in Persia. By the end of the fourth century, many pagan temples had been destroyed and earlier forms of paganism were rapidly dying out.

The change in the situation, whereby the Church was now accepted, presented new problems or accentuated old ones. There was an influx of many former pagan ideas, which did not easily fit in with the strong Hebraic background of the early days. For nearly three hundred years, the Church of Rome was a Greek colony in its language, organisation, writers, scriptures and liturgy. This powerful Greek influence inevitably resulted in many compromises, not only in beliefs but also in practices. The pressure of secular society grew when the recognition of the Christian religion gave temporal power to Church leaders whose areas were designated by titles which approximated to those of local civil or military governors. In many cases, political authority was given to Church leaders, who were often the chosen advisers of emperors and rulers, because these Church leaders were the best-educated in such arts as reading and writing for the service of the Christian community and the State. A notable instance in the period of Constantine is Eusebius, bishop of Caesarea, who advised Constantine and wrote the *Historia Ecclesiastica*, which was the earliest authorised history of the Church.

The changes in the Christian community took many forms. Worship became more elaborate as it received wider recognition; diocesan bishops attended the courts of kings (even though they might rebuke them) and the hierarchy of class distinctions in society increasingly became manifest in the Church. It was also now possible to exert the powerful arm of the civil power against heretics and ecclesiastical opponents, especially after the Nicene Creed was issued as the standard of orthodoxy in 325. (The earlier Apostles' Creed appeared at the close of the second century.) Struggles for power became scenes of bloodshed when the arm of the law could be invoked.

Nevertheless, the mission of the Church did not cease with the fact of recognition. New opportunities opened with legal rights and new groups in society came into the Church. From a very early period, the two sacraments of Baptism and the Lord's Supper (or Eucharist) were celebrated. In the latter sacrament, in particular, the original values were preserved, so that prince and slave could kneel together to receive the elements of bread and wine.

(b) *Formative Phases in Its History*

The recognition of the Christian faith by the Emperor Constantine brought freedom to spread the faith and also the doubtful advantages of privilege. Within the faith itself, there was considerable conflict as the various traditions (Hebraic and Greek) were endeavouring to come to terms in describing the major doctrines of the Church. The record of this struggle is seen in the great councils of the Church, and the fruit of them is seen in the great Creeds which emerged to serve as a buttress to the Church in ages to come. When the northern tribes moved into the Roman Empire during the fourth and fifth centuries the Church became the residuary legatee of Imperial culture, representing in the West the forces of law and order, as well as of education and culture, which had a profound influence on the invaders.

The moral condition of the Roman Empire came to have a significant impact on the Church, especially from the third century, when ascetic ideas (probably of Eastern origin) came to have an increasing influence. The loss of hope and the Stoic conception that the world was coming to a cyclic close, together with the political and social conditions (which included heavy taxation), caused many to turn towards a way of asceticism. This included preferring the celibate state to marriage. Many hermits took to the deserts in Egypt. Some indulged in self-torture to nullify their natural instincts and the number of celibate priests and nuns became a very significant proportion of the population in Catholic Christendom. It must, however, also be recognised that many monks and nuns sublimated their sex impulses and gave themselves to works of healing, the care of the poor, agriculture and to evangelism. They were also craftsmen, teachers and scholars. In fact, by their very concentration and devotion they showed the rich depths and heights of the finest human qualities.

The leadership given to the West by the Church reached new heights, under the leadership of Thomas Aquinas (1227–74), whose scholarship drew deeply upon the resources of ancient Greece, of Judaism and Arab Islam while retaining loyalty to the central truths of Christendom. With regard to the temporal authority of the Pope, guiding principles were laid down by Hildebrand, Pope Gregory VII (1073–85), who sought to ensure that the temporal princes of Europe were subject to his control. In the sphere of economics and in commerce, as well as in that of moral responsibility, the Church sought to create a society in which Christian principles were adopted. Usury was forbidden and trade was severely hampered by restrictions laid down for borrowing money.

The authority of the Pope was greater in the West, because the East had been severed from the West in 1054 and the Eastern and Western Churches had gone their separate ways. The Western Church remained firmly under the Pope until a series of blows weakened his authority. These included the character of some of the Popes, the rise of nationalism, the scandal of rival Popes (with a period of schism) and the revival of learning (known as the *Renaissance*)—all of which culminated in a great disruption in the Church about 1520, when a large part of Northern Europe broke away from allegiance to the Papacy to form national churches, with greater or lesser freedom towards the older forms of church government, ways of worship and practice. This period of disruption was also partly due to the fresh study of the New Testament documents and resulted in an emphasis on the judgment of the individual conscience. This emphasis, in turn, gave impetus to the spirit of enquiry, with momentous results in scientific fields, in geography, astronomy and in freedom of thought. From the stress on the salvation of the soul and preparation for a life beyond, there came instead an activist approach to this present life.

In the East, the older Byzantine and unreformed pattern remained in the Church in Russia as well as in the countries which were under the rule of Islam, where the Church lived on as a repressed sect. In Southern Europe the older Catholicism continued, in some cases reformed, as a powerful force. Fresh forms of Church organisation appeared in Scandinavia, in the northern part of Germany, in Holland and in most of Britain (excluding southern Ireland). These forms were simpler patterns which arose out of new interpretations of vernacular Scripture.

After the period of disruption, there arose a great variety of religious forms which were generally intolerant of one another and were often affected by political allegiances. Thus, in France, the Huguenots were regarded as a threat to the security of the French throne, and, in England, the Calvinist doctrine reinforced those who withstood Charles I, with his view of the divine right of kings. The Thirty Years War in Germany was a ghastly aftermath to the division in belief, which was made the instrument of national and personal ambition.

Calmer attitudes arose with the rise of rationalism which began (in Britain) at the close of the seventeenth century and continued into the early nineteenth century. The enmity of Christian bodies towards one another died away as their energies became directed towards wider fields of missionary expansion overseas. Coercion was abandoned, although there still remained a strong link between national interests and the missionary cause in Africa and the Far East. New movements arose also in the Church, such as Methodism in Britain in the eighteenth century and the Oxford Movement in the nineteenth century and these brought fresh waves of initiative and enterprise. Literary criticism and the discoveries of Near Eastern manuscripts have caused a reassessment of the Christian documents and especially of the Gospels.

(c) *Aspects of Modern Developments*

During the nineteenth century, missionary enterprise took the Christian message into areas which had largely remained untouched by Western influences. David Livingstone, Robert Moffatt, and Mary Slessor are examples of those who penetrated into Africa, while Henry Martyn and William Carey went to India and Robert Morrison to China. These missions were centres of manifold activity. They were primarily concerned with evangelism (the proclamation of the Gospel message), but this involved education, medicine and the establishment of the institutional Church in the form of that branch of the Church which had sent the missionaries.

Education was not a simple matter of sending teachers and providing buildings and equipment. There were no textbooks and, in many cases, there were no written languages, except classical texts in India and China, where only the *literati* were in a position to read them. There was no written language for the common people. Therefore, to provide the Bible in the language of the people meant that a language in writing had to be made, either in letters or in other symbols, in a script which was acceptable in the area. As a result, when the British and Foreign Bible Society came into being in 1804, the Bible had been translated into less than 400 languages in the previous centuries, whereas since that date the Bible has been produced in part in over 1300 languages. Other literature was also necessary, so Christian literature societies came into being to translate hymns and Christian classical literature (*Pilgrim's Progress, The Confessions of St Augustine, The Imitation of Christ by* Thomas à Kempis and other works). The building of schools became necessary to cater for the growing numbers of those who were interested in the new learning from the West, which included a large curriculum (history, geography, etc.) far beyond Bible subjects.

Since 1910, there has been within the non-Roman Churches an increasing attempt to explore ways for the various Christian denominations to work together and, where possible, to effect complete union. The pressure came from the 'Younger Churches' in Africa and Asia, where a disunited Church hindered the progress of mission, because tribes formerly united in religious practice became divided between Christian denominations with different or even competitive practices. The movements towards union have borne fruit in the United Church of Canada (Congregational, Presbyterian and Methodist) in 1926, in the Methodist Church in Great Britain (of three Methodist Churches) in 1932, and in the United Church of South India in 1947 (in which for the first time since the Reformation episcopal and non-episcopal Churches were brought together into one Church).

This movement has continued, and discussions are now taking place between the Methodist Church in Great Britain and the Church of England with the intent to seek complete union in two stages, while in the same country the Presbyterian and Congregational Churches are due to enter into a full Covenant of union in 1971. At the same time the Roman Catholic Church, after the Second Vatican Council, has set up a Secretariat of Christian Unity to discuss union with the 'separated Christians' of other communions and has undergone other changes, including a wider use of the Mass in vernacular languages.

There has also been an increase in the administrative machinery whereby different Churches can work together. Within countries, National Councils (like the British Council of Churches) have been established, and these national councils have become affiliated with the wider World Council of Churches, which brings together most Protestant and Orthodox communions of the Church, with Roman Catholics as observers.

Apart from these discussions with regard to organisation, there have taken place new movements in liturgical reform and in theology, which have brought together scholars of different Christian communions, and also those outside the Church. Dialogue has increasingly been taking place between believers of different religions, not only in matters relating directly to religion but by historians of religion, sociologists and anthropologists, whose interests have been more academic than doctrinal, and who have thrown fresh light on the place of religion in human affairs.

On the other hand, the advance of Marxist Communism

in areas, especially in Europe, where the Roman Catholic Church formerly held allegiance, has had a profound impact on the Church, in reducing its numbers and lessening its influence in social and political affairs. In countries devoted to Catholicism (such as Italy and Spain), the influence of Communism has had a marked anti-clerical character and has weakened the work of the Church. New currents of thought, especially of humanism (which has emphasised the capacities of the human mind), have stimulated and fascinated many of the finest minds in society, so that all branches of the Church have suffered a shortage in recruits for the ministry. In Eastern Europe, the Orthodox Church has sought to recover ground lost in the Marxist-Lenin advance, yet severe restrictions on its life and work continue. Many of its buildings have been taken over by the state and its wealth has been seized. This process has taken place wherever national policies have moved in a Marxist direction and is liable to reduce still further the material resources of the Church.

It is to be expected that the influence of the Church will find its authority to lie in its moral claim to an allegiance wider than a national one—a supra-national community under God. Its standards have withstood many a shock and its charter of love has yet to find a fuller and more complete expression.

Summary

The historical aspect of Judaism has proved a great strength as a means of survival. The rock-like quality which devotion to the Law has given to the Jewish community has enabled the widespread Dispersion of that community in many lands to weather countless storms to the infinite blessing of mankind. The peculiar circumstance of their determination to retain their identity, in the midst of other nations, has contributed to qualities of mind and character, manifest in the fields of scholarship as well as in commerce, banking and industry.

Such devotion also served as the rock on which the early Church came to be built. The strong community life, which gave a real place to the individual yet reinforced his corporate faith, enabled the slave and merchant to retain his Christian beliefs in the time of persecution and flight from city to city.

When the day of recognition came for the Christian Church, the challenge of wealth and power proved perhaps a greater test than the earlier period of poverty and persecution. The patterns of society and the currents of thought in contemporary society have always been stamped on the thinking and practice of the Church. Yet it has retained its body of doctrine, its distinctive rites and behavioural patterns, which continue to serve as a light and a guide to many different types of people, in many different cultures, in many lands. Its impact has often served to break into earlier patterns and create conflict but it has also served to be a reconciling influence, to provide a stimulus to education and healing and to quicken new currents of thought in the East and in the West. Its power of survival will be proved in its ability to face the questions raised especially by the culture, of which it was itself the matrix, in the technological West.

Appendix I

PHILOSOPHICAL RELIGION

1. Introduction

Religon has many aspects. It may be individual (as seen in the hermit and the mystic) or highly social (as in the tribal ceremonies and public acts of worship). It may be strongly emotional ('Early religion was danced out rather than thought out', wrote R. R. Marett) or it may be powerfully intellectual (as in the philosophical thought of the Indian Vedic period). It may be closely identified with human behaviour or be fixed on the transcendental mysteries of an Absolute Being. All these aspects are like the manifold facets of a jewel. They are reflected also in the varieties of definition of 'religion', so that Professor Leuba gathered forty-eight different definitions in his *A Psychological Study of Religion.*

It is therefore clear that no narrow interpretation can be given to the term 'religion'. It involves a relationship to the Ultimate Values (however conceived), which embraces the whole psychic life of a person, who is at the same time individual yet part of a social context. The Ultimate Values may be conceived in terms of a relationship between man and some power or powers higher than himself or, in other terms, as loyalty to Ultimate Truth, to a Process or to Humanity (as the final duty of man). With the development of the intellectual life of men, it is to be expected that the claims of the intellect to conceive the Ultimate Goal for mankind should not be lightly dismissed. In fact, attention should be given to philosophical goals, which are deemed to be *ultimate* and as such fill the place of a religious demand in the lives of many men and women. It is a *Way* or *Cause* which calls forth all their powers as of infinite worth, which receives devotion similar to that which is offered to a deity.

2. Development

From early times, thinking man has reflected on the ultimate meaning of the world in which he lives. This reflection is concerned with life and death and the issues of human endeavour, which are all part of that ultimate mystery, which in other religions finds focus in the term 'God'. While many of the thinkers would deny that they believe in a god or gods and in many cases would regard themselves as atheist, yet their concern for the ultimate goals of life bring their thought into the sphere of 'religion'.

It was in early Greece, from the sixth century B.C. onwards, that questions began to be asked about the nature of the mystery of the world. An early physicist, such as Thales (*c.* 585 B.C.), believed that the ultimate substance was water and he and his followers recognised that whilst change was self-evident, yet behind all things there seemed to be an underlying unity. Some writers stressed the element of continual change, as did Heracleitus, who believed that the element Fire embodied the fact of change. He believed that all changes took place through the influence of fire, so all things are relative and nothing is fixed. Others stressed the factor of permanence, as did Xenophanes (570–480

B.C.) who sought to replace the older polytheistic beliefs by a belief in an immutable and all-embracing material universe. The nature of the physical universe occupied much of their speculation but it was also realised that reason (in man) needed to be separated from material elements. Anaxagoras (500–429 B.C.) asserted the supremacy of Mind over all other elements in the universe, although he still gave primary attention to the interaction of physical elements, such as earth, air and water. The difference between things and thought exercised many minds, even though only a few of their writings have come down to us.

The concentration on the nature of material things led logically to the belief that all things are in fact material, which found expression in the writings of Democritus, who reduced everything to atoms, which were differentiated between senses and thought; but both were regarded as material. Perception was outward through the senses and inward through processes of thought, but both were activities of absolute matter expressed through atoms which he held to be fundamental.

This ancient conception has raised its head at various times across the centuries as a 'naturalist' explanation of the facts of the physical universe. It regards all phenomena as the coming together of physical elements. Man is the result of physiological or psychical and physical factors, but even his purposes are explained as the result of different chemical components reacting to the environmental situation. The place of values and spiritual insights is difficult to explain in this view because Shakespeare, for example, is not easily explained as merely chemically different from his fellows. The flashes of insight and of genius may well spring from an inner connection with a larger world which man perceives at particular times and with which he communicates from time to time through religion, ideals and moral purposes.

The other great difficulty about a materialist explanation of the true nature of life lies in the fact of consciousness, which has the feeling of freedom. In a fully materialistic universe, the elements are determined and the freedom of the will is an illusion. This again comes into collision with man's sense of responsibility and with his ideals, which cannot be so easily explained away. Materialism is a cold comfort to human life and has mainly appealed to intellectuals, who wish to deal with life in terms of logic, omitting emotion, imagination and other factors which play a large part in every human life.

The philosopher's goal may be sought in other directions. He may begin with phenomena, which are the object of our senses, and then seek to reach out beyond things seen and touched to the ideas which lie behind them. The great philosophers of Greece were aware of the function of human reason and human ideals in the understanding of things.

Plato believed in a world of Ideas which stood apart from Matter, but Matter reflected in part the world of Ideas. We see a 'table', but the perfect table lies in the world of Ideas. Aristotle begins from the other end. We have the table (our starting point) and by reason we reach out to the perfect object. So in the world of Ideas, he sought to find ultimate meaning in an Absolute Unmoved Mind—an ideal towards which the whole process in creation moved. Such a conception had logical satisfaction but lacked any flesh and blood warmth about it, so that it provided no help to the mass of mankind who needed some emotional satisfaction beyond the appeal of the intellect.

From these two philosophers, there have stemmed two main branches of human thought. Those who follow in the train of Plato begin with the Idea of the Perfect and then deduce the patterns which are found in the everyday world. Mind is the most important factor and these philosophers are known as *Idealists*, proceeding from Mind to Material. On the other hand, there are those who begin from the world of phenomena and seek to induce facts about Mind and reason from the actual world of sense. These are known as *Realists*, who have their modern representatives in the scientific world, proceeding from fact to fact to build up the classification of human thought, without bringing in mysteries which are not easy to classify, such as are found in religion, art and imagination.

3. The Place of Reason

The place of human reason came to receive increasing attention. While man shares much with the animal creation, it is evident that he has capacities which raise him above the animals. Thus, in Aristotle, we find that he extols *Virtue* as the supreme end of man's life and as the voluntary unobstructed realisation of man's rational nature. In the preceding century, Confucius (about the year 500 B.C.) extolled the nature of the *Princely Man*, who was governed by reason and harmonious relationships. The development of this praise for human intelligence led to the 'humanistic' thought, which sees man as the goal of creation. This emphasis sees in the human mind the ultimate mystery beyond which there is no need for a deity. The evolutionary process is considered to find its fulfilment in the full development of the human capacities, which will enable all things in creation to be rightly ordered.

It may well be claimed that such concepts of philosophers should not be regarded as aspects of 'religion'. Confucius, in China, disclaimed any measure of inspiration and regarded himself as a teacher of morals. However, his teaching in due time filled the place of religion in many lives. There can hardly be found any city in China which is without a temple dedicated to him and while philosphers may not be worshipped as divine beings, yet their teaching can fill an intellectual vacuum for those who find much contemporary religion (in whatever century) to be tasteless or lacking in depth. Through the influence of Aristotle and, later, through the Stoics (especially as represented by such noble figures as Seneca and Marcus Aurelius), there passed a line of thought which came to a flowering in the conception of Renaissance Man—the fully human personality (well equipped in body, mind and spirit). In the eighteenth century, the Age of the Enlightenment gave added emphasis to this concept.

The growth of scientific terms, to measure and classify all kinds of objects, has gradually pushed back the frontiers of the area of the unknown. When the cause of an event was not known, it was previously attributed to the divine and this hindered scientific advance, because, in some cases, further research into hidden causes was regarded as impious or as undermining the faith of believers. The established orthodoxy of traditional faith frowned on investigations which threatened to throw into doubt the long-accepted beliefs of the Church. Thus, there grew up a deep opposition between those who thought in scientific terms and those who cherished the theology of the Church.

The growth of this opposition may be seen by contrasting the age of Isaac Newton and Robert Boyle (at the close of the seventeenth century), when scientists were also devout

Christian believers, and the mid-nineteenth century, when the open clash took place between Christian orthodoxy (expressed by the Bishop of Oxford) and the new believers in evolution, whose protagonists were Charles Darwin and Thomas Huxley. In France, Germany and also in England, there arose a deep hostility between those who sought to open the flood-gates of new scientific ways and those who feared such flood waters, lest the ancient faith should be submerged.

For those who rejected the authority of the Church, it is probably true that most of them did not reject entirely belief in God (although some did), but they remained agnostic—those who did not know. For such agnostics, it was easier to fall back on the known—a belief in the potentiality of man, whose abilities were being so strikingly revealed in the wonders of the industrial and scientific discoveries. Man was seen to be both the measure and the master of things, so any belief in God could be pushed back to the circumference, except for those who still found value in the idea.

The continual expansion of scientific and technological knowledge has strengthened the belief of many 'humanists', who have held firmly to the ability in man to meet the demands made by his own achievements. However, there have been some doubts cast on this belief by the dangers inherent in man's nature. Two world wars, the organised propaganda and concentration camps of National Socialism and the continual conflicts across the world certainly do not give any ground for a facile belief in man's ability to cope with the world. The older liberalism with its optimistic idea of progress—that the world would get better and better in progressive stages—has received a severe set-back.

Among the scientists, there has been a growing questioning about their moral responsibility for the results of their discoveries—as they feel unable to stand by and watch the fall-out of atomic materials, which may have severe repercussions not only on the contemporary world but on future generations.

The call for some form of moral criterion becomes more insistent as a touchstone in permitting new knowledge to be made available to developing nations. The claim for science among these new nations has almost amounted to a new religion of 'scientism', wherein man's achievements become ends in themselves. The separation from 'other-worldly' claims, as expressed in religion, is emphasised by the term 'secularism', which claims that 'man has come of age' and no longer needs any criteria beyond the human to guide him in the use of his possibilities.

These claims—many of which deny belief in any form of God—are all part of the movement of the spirit of man and express views of the ultimate goal of man. As ultimates, these views may be held to be religious, serving as a comprehensive hypothesis not only for academic and philosophical purposes but also for moral guidance and for spiritual goals of beauty and goodness.

One of the most significant movements of the present time is that of the Marxist-Leninist belief in the conception of Dialectical Materialism. Karl Marx retained his Jewish heritage of Messianic mission, when he sought to discover laws in social and economic history as a guide to human destiny. The victory of the proletariat served for him as the fulfilment of the community of the faithful. The passion for the cause, the devotion to leaders and the practices of Marxist Communism have for many people taken the place of a religion. In China, the new interpreter is Mao Tse-Tung, but the emphasis on a rational and materialistic approach finds many followers there, where much Confucianist thought tends in a similar direction. The aim of the movement is to find a way of life for the masses, whose lot for many centuries has been shackled by traditional ways of thought and practice.

The massive achievements in Soviet Russia provide a word of hope for other peoples who are backward in technological achievement. It is not therefore a matter for surprise that African States have found such an example a glowing one to follow. Yet, for the mass of the people, philosophical concepts have little appeal. Their emotions and the mystery of life itself call for some further Self-Existent, to whom prayer and worship can be offered. It is apparent that an intellectualism or an anti-clericalism which sought to sponsor Anti-God Movements in Russia did not quench the quest for religion in the hearts of men. It is therefore to be expected that a more intellectual form of faith will arise for those who remain unsatisfied by traditional beliefs, but it remains an object of conjecture as to the forms of faith and practice which will continue to meet the demands of the ordinary believer in Russia, China and other nations in the East and West.

Appendix II

MYSTICISM

WHILE the term 'religion' has often been interpreted in terms of rational belief, it is evident that some aspects of religious expression may give only a comparatively small place to reason. It was claimed, for example, by the French anthropologist Lèvy-Bruhl, that primitive man was 'pre-logical' in his activity and lived in a sense of mystic communal 'belonging', not only with his fellows but with all nature. Evidence was drawn from totemism and other rites to uphold such a theory. However, the investigations of B. Malinowski, Raymond Firth and other social scientists have shown that such pre-logical thinking is not evident even in very primitive tribes, where the skilled elders show great competence as gardeners and fishermen within the limits of their experience. They are also great weathermen for the purposes of agriculture.

Moreover, even though the social instinct or gregariousness is most prominent in tribal life, there is also a place for the solitary individual. This individual may be separated by curious idiosyncrasies, such as the neurotic or epileptic (of a physical nature), or by a temperament which delights in solitude, as in the case of some hermits. In solitude, various 'religious' experiences take place which serve as a guide to future practice. Such solitary men or women are often sought out for the guidance which it is believed that they are able to give. In such solitaries, there lies the origin of the idea of 'mysticism', which has come to be recognised as present in most faiths, even though the use of the term itself is comparatively modern.

While the philosopher seeks truth by the use of reason and the intellect, other thinkers have sought the ultimate goal through a union of thought and feeling, which is expressed in the concept of 'mysticism'. All religions, in all their various stages of development, have some aspect of mysticism, which finds particular expression through prophets and shamen in early forms of religion as well as through the more highly developed forms of the famous mystics of more culturally advanced faiths.

In the early tribal religions, most young men were expected to have some mystic experience—as may be seen most clearly among the American Indian peoples. When the Iowa brave went into retreat to prepare for his visionary experience, he was instructed by the medicine man to realise the social and religious importance of his experience. In his experience, there was a significant union of social status, deepened spiritual awareness and moral values, which did not arise solely out of social origin. Similarly, in South Africa, in the Sudan, and in New Zealand, particularly in the nineteenth century, there were developments of prophetism, which blended social protest, emotional reaction to events and also moral and spiritual elements, often of high quality.

The primitive prophet or seer 'stands midway between the mystic and the medium',* so that, together with the elements of emotion (in periods of trance, ecstasy and even ravings), there are also elements of an intellectual nature

* Christopher Dawson, *Religion and Culture* (London, 1949), p. 71.

and sometimes of deep moral insight, in the guidance he gave to individuals or to his people. Vision and inspiration were rated as the most exalted forms of knowledge among tribal peoples, and the prophets (as an élite) were accorded an important place in society.

Prophetic vision has large elements of emotion contained in it, so that it appeared to be contagious, whether in the dances of witch-doctors or in the Near Eastern Dionysiac enthusiasm or in the schools of the Israelite prophets to which reference is made in the Old Testament. This experience was not confined to those of a particular class of society, although it is apparent that the office of a shaman or medicine man often ran in families. The 'neurotic' signs which marked out a man or woman as a medium were sought among his sons or nephews to discover the one who was the designated (i.e. designated by the gods) successor. This practice continues among the Red Indian tribes in North America today, however much education and social recognition a man may have in normal American society. A graduate of three universities who serves as the medicine man of his tribe among the Cherokee Indians told me about the signs evident in his third son (a ten-month-old birth, some nervous signs and temperamental traits), by which the tribe was already agreed that this child was due to be his father's successor—although the child was under three years old.

Prophetism is an important element in Islam which continues to be influenced by prophetic movements, some of which are in modern times regarded as religious societies as in Egypt. Such movements are in part the reaction and revolt against the strict legal character of Islam. There has arisen, in particular, the variety of mystics, especially in

Persia, who are grouped together in Muslim circles under the term 'Sufi'. While the meaning of the word is not certain, it is probable that it refers to the white woollen garment (*suf*) worn by mystical ascetics, although the term may also be connected with the Greek term for wisdom (*sophia*). Greek influences may in fact have entered into the early Islamic world and found expression in the teaching of Islamic mystic teachers.

It is commonly believed that all mystics (of culturally advanced faiths)—whether Buddhist, Hindu, Muslim or Christian—agree on certain fundamentals, such as the unreality of separateness, the illusory nature of evil and the unreality of time. These three concepts certainly play a large part in the thinking of many mystics.

With regard to the first, all division is regarded as unreal in a universe which forms one single indivisible unity. Therefore, it is the mystic's quest to seek that inner unity, which removes the veils of transitory separateness.

With regard to the second, the illusion of evil is held to arise from the attempt to consider a part of creation as separate and self-subsistent, when the underlying unity is denied.

In the third concept, the true experience of reality is believed to be outside time, so that time itself is in fact unreal. To enter the inner reality is to share in timelessness.

It is important, however, to keep certain distinctions clear in the understanding of the mystic experience. In the first place, there are certain temperaments to whom this type of experience makes a particular appeal. It may even be claimed that in some it may well be a gift (in the same way as an ability in music or in languages in others). It is therefore unwise to regard such an experience as a higher type of religion or as superseding other types of religious experience. Secondly, there are distinct attitudes within mysticism according to the different theological approaches of the individual mystics. There are for example main streams which can be detected within the Christian mystic tradition, and it is to be expected that in other religions, such as in Hinduism, there are distinct mystic traditions, which vary according to the approach to deity which is conceived in personal or non-personal terms. The doctrine of creation is also involved in the understanding of the mystic experience.

It is therefore to be expected that the Christian and Muslim mystics will vary greatly in their approach to deity. The truly Christian form of mysticism accepts the Hebraeo-Christian doctrine of an active deity, who has made a world which is good and who works in and through time. It is also part of this tradition that the experience of communion with God will be through the Risen Christ, which was well expressed in the words of St. Paul: 'I live, yet not I, but Christ liveth in me'. Similarly, in Teresa of Avila, the experience came in terms of the Trinity. It is not to be expected that the Muslim will approach deity in such ways or find such expression for his religion. In fact, within the Christian tradition, great influence has been exercised by a bogus work, known now as *Pseudo-Dionysius*, which stemmed from Indian and Greek thought, and became a text book for many leading mediaeval Christian mystics, such as Johannes Eckhart and Henry Suso. Its ideas were only superficially Christian and in many cases (e.g. in the view of evil) inconsistent with the New Testament. Such teaching had wide vogue as *Neo-Platonism*, both within Christianity and beyond it, in Islamic mysticism.

Outside Christianity, mysticism has had an important place in the religion of India. Numerous parallels have been drawn with the sayings of Hindu and Buddhist saints as close to those of Christian mystics, yet this may often have been due to a common source of apocryphal writing, such as that of the Levantine pagan mystic Proclus, whose work was made available to those in the East and the West. Mysticism has not had an easy home in Islam. It had a prominent place in mediaeval Judaism, being represented in the group known as the Kabbalists. The diffusion of similar mystical ideas over wide areas appears to explain the presence of like techniques and doctrines in widely scattered places, to which the ideas travelled and found a fruitful soil.

BIBLIOGRAPHY

Introduction

A. C. BOUQUET, *Comparative Religion*. London, Penguin, 1965.
M. ELIADE and J. KITAGAWA, *The History of Religions*. Chicago, 1959.
J. MURPHY, *The Origin and History of Religions*. Manchester, 1949.
R. C. ZAEHNER (ed.), *The Concise Encyclopaedia of Living Faiths*. Hutchinson, 1959.

Pre-Literary Religion

V. ELWIN, *The Religion of an Indian Tribe*. Oxford, 1955.
E. O. JAMES, *Prehistoric Religion*. Thames & Hudson, 1957.
H. FRANKFORT and others, *Before Philosophy*. Pelican, 1954.
W. KOPPERS, *Primitive Man and his World Picture*. Sheed & Ward, 1952.
E. G. PARRINDER, *African Traditional Religion*. Hutchinson, 1954.

India

A. C. BOUQUET, *Hinduism*. Hutchinson, 1948.
C. HUMPHREYS, *Buddhism*. Pelican, 1951.
N. MACNICOL, *Living Religions of the Indian People*. S.C.M., 1934.
K. W. MORGAN (ed.), *The Religion of the Hindus*. Ronald Press, N.Y., 1953.
K. M. SEN. *Hinduism*. Pelican, 1961.
J. JAINI, *Outlines of Jainism*, 2nd ed. Cambridge, 1940.
KHUSHWANT SINGH, *The Sikhs*. Allen & Unwin, 1953.

China

WING-TSIT CHAN, *Religious Trends in Modern China*. New York, 1953.
E. R. and K. HUGHES, *Religion in China*. Hutchinson, 1950.
K. L. REICHELT, *Religion in Chinese Garment*. Lutterworth, 1951.
W. E. SOOTHILL, *The Lotus of the Wonderful Law*. Oxford, 1930.
A. WALEY, *The Way and Its Power*. Allen & Unwin, 1934.
LIN YU TANG, *The Wisdom of China*. Joseph, 1949.

Japan

M. ANESAKI, *Religious Life of the Japanese People*. Tokyo, 1938.
D. C. HOLTOM, *The National Faith of Japan*, New York, 1938.
H. THOMSEN, *The New Religions of Japan*. Tokyo, 1963.
B. L. SUZUKI, *Mahayana Buddhism*, 2nd ed. Marlow, 1948.
P. WHEELER, *The Sacred Scriptures of the Japanese*. Allen & Unwin, 1952.

Islam

E. E. CALVERLY, *Worship in Islam*, 2nd ed. Luzac, 1957.
N. J. DAWOOD, *The Koran*, 2nd revised ed. Penguin 1966.
K. CRAGG, *The Call of the Minaret*. Oxford, 1956.
A. GUILLAUME, *Islam*, 2nd ed. Pelican, 1956.
C. E. PADWICK, *Muslim Devotions*. S.P.C.K., 1960.
W. C. SMITH, *Islam in Modern History*. Oxford, 1957.

Judaism

I. EPSTEIN, *Judaism*. Pelican, 1959.
T. H. GASTER, *Festivals of the Jewish Year*. New York, 1952.
E. R. BEVAN and C. SINGER, *The Legacy of Israel*. Oxford, 1927.

Christianity

H. BETTENSON, *Documents of the Christian Church*. Oxford, 1943.
T. CORBISHLEY, *Roman Catholicism*. Hutchinson, 1950.
F. L. CROSS, (ed.), *Oxford Dictionary of the Christian Church*. Oxford, 1957.
E. O. JAMES, *A History of Christianity in England*. Hutchinson, 1951.
N. MICKLEM (ed.), *Christian Worship*. Oxford, 1936.
E. UNDERHILL, *Essentials of Mysticism*. Methuen, 1920.
T. WARE, *The Orthodox Church*. Penguin.

INDEX